DATE DUE

Maryalice Fairbank Miner could swim before she could walk, and has dedicated her life to coaching, teaching, and organizing programs in all disciplines in the field of aquatics. She counts her students at more than 20,000, and has coached AAU Group and interscholastic swimming and diving (producing state and national champions), produced and directed water ballet shows, helped organize the Mississippi State (Gulf Coast) Swimming and Diving Association, and specialized in teaching infants, pre-school, and distressed swimmers. Mrs. Miner is certified as a National Swim Official, is a past or present member of the American Swimming Coaches Association and the International Swimming Hall of Fame, and is listed in *Who's Who of American Women.*

Maryalice Fairbank Miner

Water Fun

Swimming Instruction and Water Games for the Whole Family

A SPECTRUM BOOK

Prentice-Hall, Inc., Englewood Cliffs, New Jersey 07632

Library of Congress Cataloging in Publication Data

Miner, Maryalice Fairbank.
   Water fun.

   (A Spectrum Book)
   Bibliography: p.
   Includes index.
   1. Swimming.   2. Family recreation.   I. Title.
GV837.M56   797.2'1   80-11647
ISBN 0-13-945824-7
ISBN 0-13-945816-6 (pbk.)

© 1980 by Prentice-Hall, Inc., Englewood Cliffs, N.J. 07632

A SPECTRUM BOOK

Printed in the United States of America

10 9 8 7 6 5 4 3 2 1

Editorial/production supervision and interior design by Maria Carella.
Manufacturing buyer: Cathie Lenard.
Cover design by Judith Kazdym Leeds.

PRENTICE-HALL INTERNATIONAL, INC., *London*
PRENTICE-HALL OF AUSTRALIA PTY., LIMITED, *Sydney*
PRENTICE-HALL OF CANADA, LTD., *Toronto*
PRENTICE-HALL OF INDIA PRIVATE, LIMITED, *New Delhi*
PRENTICE-HALL OF JAPAN, INC., *Tokyo*
PRENTICE-HALL OF SOUTHEAST ASIA PTE., LTD., *Singapore*
WHITEHALL BOOKS, LIMITED, WELLINGTON, *New Zealand*

This book is dedicated to my husband John,
and to our children, David, Steve, John, and Merileigh,
without whom it never would have happened.

Contents

Foreword

The bubbling spirit of "Bubs" (Maryalice Miner) fills this book with the magic that she lists as a trick of the trade. It's no wonder that this titian-haired little lady has inspired competitive swimmers into becoming state and national class swimmers, babies into loving the water, and all those in between into accomplishing the impossible.

When Maryalice saw that Mississippi swimming needed leadership she jumped into AAU activities and brought her family with her. Together they built pools, organized teams, and put together a state organization that brought hundreds of age-group swimmers into a going program. Olympic coaches and Olympic swimmers alike responded to her requests for clinics to help these youngsters on their way.

Water Fun: Swimming Instruction and Water Games for the Whole Family is a book for everyone because in addition to coaching Maryalice also found time to teach, and teach, and teach. Her students over the past two and a half decades number over twenty thousand. This book shares her secrets and experiences with those who read it. The concern, joy, and willingness to aid the swimmer that have made her a legend in her own time are obvious on every page. Read it and be a family of happy swimmers with her!

JACK W. NELSON
1972 Women's Olympic
Swim Coach **xi**

Preface

Water Fun will teach you everything from how to get rid of Monster Fear to how to teach yourself and your baby to swim.

Chapter 1 not only builds your confidence but separates fact from fallacy so you will understand all about a different environment—water.

The ABCs of stroke work are explained in Chapter 2. I share the secrets that I have learned in twenty-five years of teaching swimming. Psychology, a knowledge of motor development, technical expertise, and obvious delight in the subject weave a magic spell that convinces you that you can be a swimmer and a diver, too. Step-by-step photos and drawings explain movements in detail.

"How To Go Swimming Together and Enjoy It" gets things in order so that you can avoid those miserable outings where everything goes wrong. Where to swim, what to take with you, first aid, safety rules, and instructions for games and relays that everyone from baby to grandpa and grandma can participate in are included in Chapter 3. For a celebration or a splash party and for an activity that will keep everyone busy for days, choreography for a water show routine is outlined. Drawings and photographs will show you how.

Swimming builds a better body, and Chapter 4 covers

all the possibilities. You can plan a personalized fitness program by following the simple pulse rate workouts or by using aquaticalisthenics. Information on all competitive swimming programs will encourage and assist you if *you* or your children decide to give the competitive scene a try. And just in case you need to know how to get rid of green hair you'll find the answer here.

Extracurricular fun is just that, and when you finish Chapter 5, you will be ready to buy a boat and a house on the bay; to build a swimming pool, or at least to join the Peeping Toms who snorkel around watching the creatures of the deep.

First, last, and always, safety is necessary. The last chapter of this informative and fun-filled book sums up how to be safe while having a good time. It also answers a myriad of questions that help finish the story of becoming water wise while having water fun!

Let's Swim! Swimming is the ideal family sport because it is fun for everyone. Besides, it is good for you! It develops your strength and improves your safety. And, do you know that swimming also builds a better bustline and more beautiful legs; reduces your blood pressure as well as your stomach; and, miraculously, helps prevent varicose veins? Children who swim improve their coordination and sometimes their IQs. Their language skills benefit, and their bodies develop overall as they change from marshmallows to tough little people.

Participation is not limited by age, size, sex, or shape. Each of us can be successful in the water and can subsequently enter a world of activity that almost defies the imagination. You can visit the colorful creatures of the deep, speed along the lake on skis, sail around the world, or ride a raft down one of America's white-water rivers. Perhaps you dream of becoming an Olympic swimmer or National Champion in the breaststroke for seventy to eighty year olds. Or, maybe you would settle for skinny-dipping at midnight in your own pool!

You can do it all if you become a swimmer. Let's do it now!

xiv   I love to teach swimming, not because I was an athlete

but because it makes me feel like Santa Claus! The abso-
lute joy and confidence that fills the spirit of the tiny tot or
the senior citizen delights and excites me. My heart used to
pound when each of my competitive swimmers strained to
excel. These days are quieter, but there are times when I
have to shout, "Merry Christmas!" to a radiant little one
who has surprised himself by taking those first independent
strokes. What greater fulfillment can a teacher find than
playing Santa Claus to youngsters or directing oldsters to a
Fountain of Youth?

Use this book as your guide to Christmas or Eternal
Youth!

MARYALICE FAIRBANK MINER
Ocean Springs, Mississippi

Come on in! The water's fine!

Acknowledgements

Writing this book has been an interesting experience for my whole family. My husband John, who has designed and provided me with swimming pools for so many years, has helped, whenever I needed him, with every aspect of its production. Our son David brought his wife Barbara and his son Mike and baby Robert from Houston to re-enact some scenes from his youth. John also came from Texas to join in the fun. Steve served as major consultant, as well as being one of my photographers. Debbie, his wife, has typed, cooked, and heaven knows what else. Daughter Merileigh, my cheerful and capable assistant, has worked beyond the call of duty as model, secretary, housekeeper, and instructor. My first thanks for their unfailing support and encouragement during my "authoritis" are to my family.

Jo Ippolito Christensen convinced me to write it all down and has helped me step by step. Emily Suares and Diane Krogstad met with me weekly all winter to make certain I kept my schedule. Prep school All-American Kirk Hale posed for the stroke pictures. Jack Nelson of Fort Lauderdale, Florida, wrote the Foreword. Many of my little people and their parents came "extra" to make the pictures possible. Joanne Anderson answered my calls for help when I got stuck, as well as helping with proofreading; Ginny Howkins also proofread for me. Peggy George typed the final copy of the manuscript. Thanks to all of you for the

ACKNOWLEDGEMENTS tangible contributions you have so willingly made. Thanks also to the Royal D'Iberville Hotel, formerly the Sheraton-Biloxi, for the use of their beautiful pools. Intangible contributions have been made by many, especially by Jim "Doc" Counsilman, Dick Bower, Dick Kimball, George Haines, Hobie Billingsley, Dave Robertson, Ed Smyke, John Foster, and, again, Jack Nelson. These men are all world-class coaches who have shared their knowledge and skill with me during many years. Without it I never would have been a coach. Thank you, gentlemen!

Kathi Winther, a doctorate student in motor development at Louisiana State University, came from Baton Rouge to help me calculate training pulse rates for the fitness programs in "Build a Better Body." Kathi and I had a movement education kindergarten for several years and working with her again was delightful. We couldn't resist getting in the water to "play," the result of which was the choreography for Blue Hawaii, the water show routine in "How To Go Swimming Together and Enjoy It." Thank you, Kathi, for all your contributions.

Chris Kent, I thank you for being lighthearted enough to do my drawings. Steve Rusk, I thank you for your wife, child, ready camera, and hard work.

Gabriele Boike, chief photographer, I thank you for giving up your normal existence for two months to join me in a difficult search for perfection. I also thank your husband David for supporting you as diligently as my family has supported me.

1

How to Overcome Fear and Gain Confidence

Almost everyone is afraid of new and different things. There is nothing wrong with being afraid, but there is no need to stay that way. This section tells you how to get rid of your fears and build confidence. It also deals with giving confidence to your children and others with whom you swim.

Figure 1-1. *Confidence supreme.*

Fear

Chances are that if you are an adult nonswimmer, you are afraid. So let's start with fear and see what we can do to get rid of it.

"What do YOU know about it?" my defensive grown-ups ask.

Teenage boys, far bigger than I, have gripped my neck and screamed in terror at their first deep-water swim.

Trembling old ladies have held my hands as we walked back and forth repeatedly in three and one-half feet of water.

Young mothers' eyes have filled with tears when I have asked them to show their babies how to pick the jelly beans off the underwater steps.

Little boys and little girls, rigid and feverish with fright, have sat on the side and watched me with their happy peers for days before joining us at play.

Except for the babies, most of my students come to me because they are afraid. They have made the momentous decision to rid themselves of that heart-stopping, suffocating, nauseating monster—FEAR.

They have taught me about fear.

Fear is unquestionably a miserable feeling, and fear of the water is much more common than one would suppose. Sometimes it is the result of a truly bad experience, and occasionally it is due to thoughtless conversation, tall tales, and lack of knowledge. We are all fearful, concerned, and cautious about new things, and, certainly, water is a totally different environment.

To adapt to it, knowledge is essential. To paraphrase an old truism, familiarity breeds content.

Babies are *not born afraid of the water.* They are born with a fear of falling, and many of my little people have commented to me that they are afraid that they will fall to the bottom of the pool and stay there. Hence, it is my opinion that the real problem is not the water itself but the lack of understanding that the water, no matter how deep, will hold the swimmer up if the swimmer will *let* it! Plan all your activities and progressions so there will be no feelings of falling. Bouncing, dropping, dangling come after a person feels good in the water.

Many people are not really afraid, but they just "don't like to put their faces into the water." They feel as if they are going to suffocate.

It is worth whatever practice, trickery, bribery, and time it takes to get over this feeling, because in any water emergency, the head is going to go underwater. Also, the most dependable survival skills involve putting your face underwater. To help yourself get used to having your face in the water:

- Learn to hold your breath (no bubbles yet).
- Put your nose in the water first, *decisively!*
- After your face is in the water, *open your eyes.*

4 Practice this in the bathtub *every day.* Start showing your

children how to put their faces in the water before they are a
year old, and do it with them.

Some people are uneasy even when walking in the water. This is because our natural buoyancy upsets normal balance and changes normal gravity. Watch youngsters walk the first few times they are in the pool. See how they tip-toe or take giant steps or wobble. If you feel yourself doing those things, too, just practice walking in the water. Everyone will benefit from a little experience.

Because of the personalized attention I give my students and because of small classes that I teach, nearly all the adults who come to me have had traumatic experiences and are honestly frightened. Most of their bad fear stems from having been thrown into the water by a "sink-or-swim" advocate or from having been forced under water. Some experts recommend fifteen or twenty forced submersions to teach the student to adapt to the water. I STRONGLY DISAGREE with them. It is the responsibility of the instructor (mother, father, sister, brother etc.) to encourage the swimmer to *want* to go underwater. The parents should help by encouraging the child at home and also by going underwater themselves. Everyone must go underwater, but not by force. I have found that if we discuss these fears and acknowledge them, it is very possible to find satisfactory, mutually agreeable ways to get rid of them.

Children, on the other hand, are so self-concerned that discussing fears with them can become self-defeating. I never ask a child if he is afraid. I feel him. If he is feverish, clammy, tense, or overtalkative, it is obvious. I don't need to ask him. If he tells me, "I'm scared," I say, "Okay, that's all right. You are smart to be afraid of something that you don't know anything about. Let me help you and teach you about the water. Then you won't have to be afraid." Just accept confessed fear as a sensible, normal feeling. Don't say, "there's nothing to be afraid of," "what are you afraid of," "I've got you," or anything else that will reinforce or magnify the fear. Listen to what children tell you; you can learn a lot.

A few children, and adults too, think that drowning is instantaneous or that one choke or sniff will wipe a guy out. Frequently, a pupil will tell me that he "drowned already." A little girl told me a very serious story about the time she jumped off the diving board with her mother and "went 5 down to the bottom and drowned." I asked her what she did about it, and her answer was, "got out and blew my nose and wiped my eyes." Some other revealing definitions include: "Drowning is what happens if you are out in a boat and someone pulls the plug!" "Drowning happens when you fall in with your clothes on." "Drowning makes your nose burn."

Fear definitely can be overcome by a positive combination of acknowledgment, knowledge, and patience. Keep these guidelines in mind for yourself, as well as for your children.

- Acknowledge the fear.
- Discover the source.
- Study the problem (read on).
- Take positive action (learn to swim).
- Never give up (keep trying).

I was teaching a middle-aged woman how to put her face in the water when three-year-old Catherine swam up to us. After watching the woman's sputtering and pained expressions for awhile, Catherine swam into the woman's arms and grabbed a handful of water. "Here," she said, "put a little water on your nose. Maybe that'll help!" The poor woman, she had a face full and had to accept it gracefully!

Don't Stay Afraid; Do Something about It!

The oldest person I ever taught was an eighty-seven-year-old man. A professional ice hockey player in his youth, he had been afraid to swim since his childhood. He decided to do something about it before he died. We were very successful, and swimming has brought him a great deal of pleasure for several years. He is still going strong, and feels happy with himself.

Confidence

What Is It?

Confidence is vital to all of us. It is the result of repeated **6** satisfactory experiences. The secret of attaining it is to progress gradually, learning and practicing skills in logical order.

In the water confidence is basically the ability to go underwater and not get water up your nose. It is opening your eyes and being able to see where you are. It is knowing how to pick your feet up and float. It is knowing how to put them back on the bottom without feeling awkward. It is jumping in, knowing you can turn around and swim back. Confidence is understanding what happens to you in the water and knowing how you can apply basic scientific principles and logic to make it easier to float or to swim.

Developing confidence is sometimes tricky business. It is like a "con game." You have to "con" yourself and your youngsters into doing things, and sometimes it takes a lot of sheer trickery. This is all legal provided you remember that the goal is confidence in oneself and confidence in the teacher, be he parent, friend, or stranger. Don't be afraid to use the so-called "crutches." It is when and how you use them that is important.

How to Get Confidence

- Start with a simple routine and simple exercises.
- Repeat. Repeat. Repeat.
- Always work in an orderly series of progressions.
- Have capable assistance when you feel ready to try different things.
- Avoid circumstances that could become dangerous.
- Swim often.
- Surround yourself with positive people.

How to Give Confidence

- Be cheerfully positive.
- Understand your students.
- Consider things from the student's viewpoint.
- Honor a refusal. Try another approach.
- Use the same progressions each lesson, adding new things at the end. (It is comforting to know what to expect.)
- Maintain body contact even if it is only a finger on the back.

- Always tell your student what he is going to do and demonstrate.
- Use the same phrase or words each time you give instructions.
- NEVER FORCE.
- BE ALERT.
- Reward the good performance. Ignore the not-so-good and poor performance. Remember it is repetition and participation that is important, not perfection.
- Never be out of reach until you *and* your student are ready.
- Realize that just one betrayal of confidence may erase all your previous good work.
- Impatience is futile.

Developing a Positive Attitude

The athletes who compete have many ways of "psyching" themselves up for their big moments. Unfortunately, the immediate goal of a ribbon, medal, or improved time is not available as encouragement for the average adult learning to swim. However, you should plan a series of goals for yourself. Plan a small reward for each little goal and a special prize for the major goal. It has been said that only a fool will do something for nothing. I agree. Most kids will do anything for a jelly bean, even go to the bottom to get it. What about you? What will it take to get you started?

Consider all the benefits. No longer will you have to sit on the sidelines while everyone else has fun. No longer will you have to be afraid to go boating, fishing, camping, or swimming. No longer will you have to refuse to go on a swimming date.

Okay, now that you have decided that you WANT to learn to swim, select your goals and determine your rewards. Get your friends and family to support you and to celebrate with you as you go along. Set a time limit, and be faithful and regular. Start your swim by reviewing. Finish it with what you like the best. Think positive thoughts. Behave positively. Surround yourself with positive people. You will be a swimmer. I'm positive!!

8

Controlling the environment is a confidence builder also. Select a place to swim that you enjoy. Pick a time of day when you feel good. Some people like early morning before problems press; others prefer evening because swimming relaxes them and makes them forget about their problems. Wear a comfortable, sporty suit that will not fall off. (Bikinis can be a nuisance). Treat yourself to a big towel and to a warm-up suit or stylish cover-up to put on when you get out. (We can't let the joggers outdo us!) LOOK LIKE A SWIMMER.

Figure 1-2. *Look like a swimmer: was a swimmer, is a swimmer, will be a swimmer.*

Music is helpful; so take your radio if you want, but swim to something smooth. And, of course, take the toys. **9**

Yes, just as I suggest that the little ones bring their ducks, balls, or dolls, I suggest that you bring mask, fins, or kickboard. Bring something to make practicing more fun or something that you can enjoy when your workout is over. Have your lesson plan written down, and limit yourself to thirty minutes. Set a good example, and try everything on your list at least five times. Select your skills from the list on pages 62–65. FEEL LIKE A SWIMMER. With yourself under control and the environment under control you will BE A SWIMMER.

All these items from goal setting to stage setting apply to the young children in the family as well as to the older siblings and parents!

A Word about Logic

Any time you have a question about why you aren't doing as well as you would like, try to answer it by applying logic. Swimming is a science. Dr. James Counsilman, several times Olympic coach and author of *The Science of Swimming,* has written at length on the subject. He clarified things for me and made me think seriously about why some actions worked and why others did not. If you have some knowledge of physics, apply it to yourself in the water; you may come up with some logical, orderly, applications. Here are some facts to keep in mind.

1. The position of the head in the water determines the position of the rest of the body.
2. Lungs full of air increase the buoyancy. Well-filled lungs rise to the surface. Inhale deeply.
3. To go forward through the water, you must pull the water backward.
4. The less resistance there is to the water, the easier it is to move.
5. Before you can take another breath of air you have to get rid of the old one. (Exhale by blowing air out *under* water with force.)
6. Regular and frequent breathing helps keep you from getting tired.
7. The arm pull provides the primary source of power for

10

all strokes. If the hand slaps the water when it enters for the pull, a great deal of power is lost on impact.

8. A quiet, long stroke is the strongest.

9. Kicking is important because it stabilizes the body and helps to maintain position during breathing.

10. If you want to go deeper down into the water, you blow air out and press *up* on the water with both hands at the same time.

11. If you want to keep your head out of the water, you must hold your breath and press *down* on the water with your hands.

True or False

1. People are born afraid of the water.
   False. The Le Boyer submersion immediately after birth relaxes and soothes the newborn, which pretty much eliminates that myth. In fact, most babies love to be in a pool or tub, especially if the temperature is 90° to 95° F.

2. It is not safe to swim after eating.
   False. It's not so much when you eat but how much and what that limits you. Swimming after a light meal should not bother anyone. A sandwich and soft drink are fine. Avoid swimming after heavy or highly spiced meals. Swimming coaches recommend that competitive swimmers eat a high carbohydrate breakfast before working out. Four ounces of orange juice and two or three pieces of toast with honey or jelly would be satisfactory.

3. If you fall into the water with your clothes on, you should disrobe immediately.
   False. Heavy shoes or boots should be removed. Other clothing provides protection against the elements and should be left on. It is weightless under water, and as long as you keep arms under water and use your survival skills, the bulk will not bother you. Some clothing makes satisfactory flotation devices (see Survival on page 54). Sneakers and sandals are necessary in the event you have a trashy bottom to contend with later.

11

4. Treading water is the most important thing to learn to save yourself in a water emergency.
False. Treading water requires a great deal of energy because you have to work so hard to keep your heavy head out of the water. The REST (see page 55) is the most important survival skill for everyone to learn.

5. Most people float naturally.
True. Properly positioned, nearly everyone floats. Almost all women float, and it is estimated that only one white man of every hundred is a sinker. The percentage of sinkers among blacks is considerably higher due to a heavier bone and muscle structure. Buoyancy is related to the amount of air in one's body. Fatty tissue and lung capacity are determining factors (see Floating on page 31).

6. To keep from falling to the bottom you must kick and pull fast and vigorously.
False. In the first place you are not likely to fall to the bottom. Proper body position and full lungs will keep almost anyone on top of the water.

7. Anybody and everybody can learn to swim.
True. Short, tall, skinny and fat, floater or rare sinker, young or old, deaf, blind, crippled or normal can all learn varying degrees of swimming skills.

8. If a child doesn't start competing by the time he is six years old, he doesn't stand a chance of excelling as a competitive swimmer.
False. It is the consensus of most motor development experts that the degree of perfection demanded by competitive techniques is not good for a child six years of age and under. They believe that he should have more time to develop dominance of hand and eye before having to become "stylized." Lots of swimming is recommended, but it is suggested that teaching on-the-side-breathing and mature stroking be delayed until the child has finished the first grade. I think swimming coaches would be happier if they could refuse to take swimmers under seven into the age-group program. By then, most are physically and emotionally ready. However, some of our truly great swimmers did not start until they were teenagers. Desire makes the difference.

9. Anesthesia, concussions, comas, and fainting spells may affect one's ability to adjust to the water.

    True. It has been my experience that many of my swimmers coming back into the water after surgery, illness, or accidents have difficulty with putting their faces back into the water for awhile or even with backstroking. Swimming breaststroke or using a heads-up crawl for awhile usually remedies the problem. I theorize that some subconscious resistance to a floating sensation causes this difficulty. The problem also occurs among beginner swimmers who have experienced the above-mentioned conditions.

10. The quickest way to get someone to swim is to take him into deep water and let him go.

    False. Although all animals swim naturally, man and apes must learn. It is cruel and totally unwise to force anyone into a sink or swim situation.

11. Most drownings are passive and go nearly unnoticed.

    True.

12. Once you have learned to swim, you never forget.

    True. But, there is not instant recall. Don't expect your baby or child to jump into the water on the first day of summer and do everything he learned last year. Nor should you expect to dive in yourself and to be able to swim 100 yards, make a rescue, and return safely. It takes a little time to get *organized* and a little more time to get *in condition.* Children should have lessons yearly until they have completed the Red Cross Junior Lifesaving course, and at least one parent should condition himself or herself well enough to rescue or assist family members if necessary.

13. Drownings in the United States number about 7,000 a year.

    True. According to figures from the *World Almanac and Book of Facts,* in 1978 6,827 people drowned in a variety of accidents. It is revealing to note that fatalities among men outnumbered those among women by six to one, and that the age group with the highest percentage of deaths was the fifteen to thirty-four group. I feel the higher number of deaths among men is due to the fact that many men who participate in boating and fishing **13** expeditions do not know how to swim as well as they think they can or do not wear their PFDs (lifejackets). It may also be that generally a man will attempt to make a rescue when it is not safe for him to do so. Just because a person took a lifesaving course at sixteen does not mean he is in condition enough or capable enough at thirty to safely execute a rescue in deep water. I urge *everyone* to stay in condition and to practice the survival and rescue skills. "Swimming well enough to save myself" is not sufficient.

2

Teaching Yourself and Your Family to Swim

First you learn a lot about "secrets" and "magic." Then, step by step you are guided through the basic steps of the crawl, the backstroke, the breaststroke, and the butterfly as well as the sidestroke and finning. These instructions will serve the six and over crowd. "Sing A Song of Swimming" is for the little people from six months to six years.

After the family is swimming, you can meet the diving board and get started on it too!

Tricks of the Trade

"Getting Psyched Up"

I like to have a few quiet moments before each day's lessons begin during which I review the problems and successes of my pupils. I recall the special needs of each one and prepare myself to meet them. This especially helps me to cope with reluctance and tears. It will really help you as a parent. If you are teaching yourself or your child, plan the period—and your reactions—in advance. Eliminate surprises! Peace!

Programming

If you will take the time to "program" your human "computer," chances are you will get a much better "read out!" Tell your child (or yourself) exactly what you want done, then watch him follow directions. We joke about putting the skills into the computer. It is particularly obvious with the routine that precedes the command, "swim." To give everyone time to get ready to go under water and swim, I always count *one, two, three.*

Figure 2-1. *Program your "computer."*

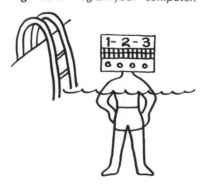

A youngster came for his first lesson of the year. His mother asked him if he remembered how to swim. "Certainly," he replied, "I'll just do it the one, two, three way—you know, I'll say one, two, three, put my face in, and swim." He did. But it was the often repeated formula that kept him organized. Always give directions in the proper sequence, repeat them a couple of times, use the same words, and limit the chain of commands to three or four. This eliminates uncertainty and improves quality. Everyone does have a computer. Just use it!

Taking Turns

Taking turns is a marvelous trick because everyone gets to watch each other. Mothers and fathers, sisters and brothers, cousins by the dozens—everybody—should get into the act. The secret is to keep it moving. Everyone has *one* chance to try the skill, then it is the next person's turn (see Figure 2-2). If an effort is made, even just a little one, clap and say, "yea." If no effort is made, go on to the next person. After a few times, the nonparticipator usually will decide he wants to be clapped for and will try. Even the babies figure this one out!

Figure 2-2. *Father and son take turns floating.*

Your attitude is very contagious. If you approach swimming with an indifferent or negative feeling, you can be sure that is the way everyone will perform. Assume everyone will try. Do not ask a child, "do you want," "do you like this," or "can you do this?" Assume he likes it and will do it and he probably will. It's hard to imagine what prompts us to ask the two year old if he "wants" to get into the pool. He has no experience on which to base a judgment.

But if we are going to assume response to our commands, we must give reasonable ones based on the readiness and capabilities of our students. Progressions must be planned so success is assured; success begets success. This is where understanding of your student, patience, and ingenuity are important. If it looks as if a routine exercise is going to be impossible for a student to master, make up a new one that he can!

Each skill should be tried, *in order,* four or five times with each swimmer executing the skill just once during his turn. This keeps the interest high and does not give anyone enough time to decide he can't do it. Resist the temptation

Figure 2-3. *See everyone watching—they are learning.*

to have one swimmer repeat the skill over and over while the others watch. Again, this is especially important in families where one child gets a lot of attention for succeeding and another gets a lot of attention ("oh please try, just once, come on," etc.) for doing nothing.

Rules

The first time I meet with a group, I explain very kindly that there are a few rules that I insist everyone obey. They are:

1. Everyone waits for permission before getting in the water.
2. Everyone stays in the pool unless he has permission to get out.
3. Everyone waits for his turn.
4. It is against the rules to say, "I can't," "I won't," or "I don't want to." It is permissible to say, "I don't know how, please show me," or "I'm scared, please help me."

The last rule produces spectacular results, if explained and enforced compassionately (*not* sympathetically). Seldom does anyone say, "I can't" more than two or three times.

Distraction

With the young children who are so very self-concerned, distraction is a helpful tool. Matter-of-fact conversation is good. It should be about familiar, unrelated things such as the child's dog. We sometimes play a talking game as we kick along or swim with the arm floats on. I'll ask what the different animals say. I still laugh when I remember Andy. He was a two year old who had not said anything to me in four weeks except a timid little "quack-quack" in response to my question, "What does the duck say?" Finally he relaxed and suddenly burst out, "and the turkey says gobble, gobble, gobble!"

Toys are a good distraction during the first lessons. Dolls are a favorite because they can take turns. We had one gigantic Raggedy Annie that helped us teach her little girl Beth to swim. Poor dollie. She was a mess after her many

20

Figure 2-4. *Toys are a good distraction.*

trips to the pool and then home to the dryer, but she was a big help!

Boats, tub toys, and balls are favorites of the babies. The older toddlers and everyone else enjoy plastic bracelets, weighted rings, hula hoops, and poker chips. Toys from home create a little security. I alternate work and play. I demonstrate the skill myself, give the student a turn at attempting the skill, and then play with the toy. If a doll, for example, is having a lesson, it takes it's "turn" before the child.

Singing Songs

Singing songs helps because it makes parents and teachers sound more pleasant. I can always tell when someone really wants to say, "Pull, dammit!' and so can the children. As the sugar helps the vinegar go down, so a song helps hide impatience. Singing is fun, and it also helps to produce movement associated with rhythm. One day I started singing to cheer up a dreary three year old. After that at each lesson she begged, "Sing song, Bubs, sing song." It worked so well for both of us that it became a habit. Be prepared to sing

21

everything from "Jesus Loves Me" to nursery rhymes, both of which are popular requests.

Humming

Did you ever try to hum and sniff water at the same time?

When you are doing the kicking drills, you can hum to your little one and then *tell him* to try it. Even six-month-olds can learn to hum. It fascinates me! Then when it is time to go underwater say, "one, two, three, *hum*" and gently release the child. Humming helps the *grown-ups* too! It eliminates some of those *painful* sniffs.

Playing School

Take turns being teacher. It's interesting to see what happens when a reluctant fellow has to give instructions and demonstrate. P. J. taught me this. He just couldn't master putting his face into the water or doing the prone float. Suddenly, I had a brainstorm. "P. J.," I said, "you know all about those things. Would you please teach your mother for me?" In explaining to his mother, he quoted me exactly and got so carried away that soon he was doing everything beautifully himself. His mother played the game well, too!

Rewards, Bribes, and Goodies

As mentioned previously, I am convinced that only a fool does something for nothing. Most babies will go underwater for a lollipop and think it's fun. Most three year olds will put their faces into the water for a jelly bean, and this works right on up the chronological ladder. My racers used to enjoy a jelly bean hunt at the end of a good workout, and women don't seem to object to playing a little peek-a-boo in exchange for a treat. After all, rats learn to spin wheels and to ring bells for a goodie, so why not modify a little human behavior with a small reward? Jelly beans and lollipops are best because they are brightly colored and don't melt. Please take safety precautions and be judicious. After a while you will need them only for special occasions, but you must reward the first few submersions immediately. Later you can provide a special treat at the end of the lesson, but deliver the goods if you've promised and if the performance

22

Figure 2-5. *Jelly bean time. Rewards help!*

warrants. I always give everybody a jelly bean for coming to class and extra jelly beans for skills done to my satisfaction. That way there is no failure for anyone.

Sometimes an outright bribe gets fantastic results, such as a new toy when the child can swim across the pool. Discuss the goal with the child and then forget it for awhile. It's not good to be constantly saying, "If you want that hamburger, you'd better hurry up and do what I say!" That's more of a threat than a promise. *Remember:* Criticism is destructive. Do not criticize unless you can demonstrate a better way.

Charts and Stars

Make a little list similar to those on pages 62–65 and 94–96 and put it on each child's (or mother's or father's) door. Each day after your swim check off the things accomplished. At the end of the week add up the checks and paste a gold star by the person's name with the most checks.

Voice-Touch

Although I have mentioned the use of the voice generally to sing songs, talk, and be cheerful, I feel it necessary to mention it again. Your voice can affect your students the very minute you speak. Practice speaking in a voice that combines authority, enthusiasm, and good will. If you sense distress, be careful not to allow sympathy to replace the **23** authority and/or the enthusiasm. Give the impression of gentle strength. If you are tired, cross, or impatient, do not let it show.

Hold your student firmly and gently. Let your confidence be *felt* as well as heard.

Attention

Most of the time it is best to give your students your total attention. If the student is your child, giving him your total attention makes him feel that you are his exclusively for a little while. Put everything else out of your mind and concentrate on having a good time learning skills together. Fortunately, or unfortunately, I concentrate so deeply that I rarely know what is going on around me while I am teaching. Really get into it and plan things so you can too.

Exceptions occur occasionally. When the two-year-olds have settled into a fairly regular routine and are not asserting their negative attitudes quite so vigorously, it may be helpful to try carrying on a relaxed conversation with someone else in the water while you physically go through the normal activities. The sound of quiet talk unrelated to himself helps soothe the child's excessive self-concern.

Knowing When to Back Down

Locking horns and waging war is no way to produce happy swimmers. Use all possible tricks to avoid battle. It can be done without embarrassment if you are alert and perceptive. Give the swimmer a choice of two things, such as swimming to the steps or going with you to get the beads off the bottom of the pool. Be sure both options are related to the skill you are working on and that they are possible. Anytime you see a "no-no" look or a look of apprehension, change the activity before your student protests loudly.

Body English

We've all seen a person backing totally out of reach of the child swimming in front of him. Stop and think about it. It is a withdrawing, nonsupportive movement. Lean forward with your hand always available (see Figure 2-6). Just the simple movement will change your child's attitude! Chances are he will not take the hand any sooner!

24

Figure 2-6. *The wake pulls the baby along unassisted.*

The wake is the little current that swirls around you as you move through the water. Boats make gigantic wakes. Swimmers make little wakes—as do people walking in the water. Youngsters need the wake you make to support them and make them feel good. Back up, move fairly fast, and let go of your child. He will ride that wake like a wave at Waikiki! Use this trick until he is so big and fast that he runs over you!

Launching

Each instructor has a method of pushing or sending a child from one person or place to another. Some teachers place a hand on the child's head, put him under water, and shove. Others simply drop their students somewhat unceremoniously in the direction of the target. I try to stick to my rule of never putting my hand on a child's head (one finger only as a signal to breathe), and I don't like the dropping technique because it makes the body go too deep into the water. I call my method launching. It is easy, the youngsters like it, and it ultimately helps teach diving. See Figures 2-7a–d and 2-36a–b. Hold the child around his legs, just above the knees. His back should be close to your stomach and chest. He will be in a standing position. Say, "one-two-three, hum" **25** and gently roll him forward until he is flat in the water. Then push gently and firmly in the direction you want him to go and release. This way you have control until he is in the

(a)

(b)

(c)

(d)

Figure 2-7a-d. *Launching.*

water. If he doesn't put his head down and get ready, you can stop and start over. He knows where he is going and what to expect, and his body position is excellent for instant swimming. It is exciting to see the six-month-olds put their heads down and get ready for this.

After a while, I call it "flying like Superman" and start with the child more out of the water. There are "big flys" and "little flys." Give the child his choice and let this be part of play time. It is the same body position used in executing shallow racing-type dives.

It's as Easy as One, Two, Three

First of all it is important to decide what you want to learn and what your goals are. Not everyone wants to learn the same things, especially at the beginning. Some want to learn survival skills. Some have the urge to look graceful in the country club pool or to have the strong, fit body that comes from exercising in the water. Decide what you want to learn first, what your goals are, and let's get started. It will make me happy if you learn anything and very happy if you decide to keep going and learn everything! See the list of goals on pages 62–65.

Water is a different environment, but most of our senses function in it anyway. We can see and hear underwater. We can touch and feel there too, but alas if we try to breathe underwater, we wish we hadn't. Sniffing water up the nose is uncomfortable but not fatal. If you go to your doctor for a nasal irrigation, you pay for it and think it's a cure for ailing sinuses. But, if you get one at your swimming lesson, it's an excuse for not learning to swim.

Obviously, the biggest differences between air and water are the lack of oxygen in the water and our buoyancy in the water. Humans can adjust to these with a little effort. It isn't terribly hard to hold your breath or to master moving through and floating in the water. Once these skills are learned, water no longer seems a strange and threatening environment (see Figure 2-8a–b.)

27

Figure 2-8a-b. *Floating.*

(a)

(b)

Go Soak Your Head (Bribe Yourself)

The very first thing that you can do to help yourself be happy in the water is to get used to putting your face into the water. The best place to learn this is in the privacy of your own tub at home! Why the bathtub? Because you can snort and cough and sputter all you want, and no one else will be around to wonder or laugh at your antics. In short you will have no worries about being embarrassed. It eliminates the excuse I hear so frequently—"I just never had a place where I could get used to putting my head under water." The tub is the **28** place and this is the way.

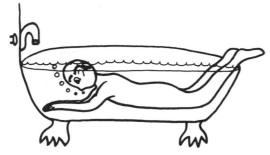

Figure 2-9. *Go soak your head!*

Fill your bathtub with warm water as deep as possible (no soap, bath oil, or bubble bath today). Get in and meditate a few minutes until you are relaxed and ready to go. Roll over on your stomach. Keep elbows and forearms on the bottom to brace yourself. Count one, two, three. Take a comfortably big breath. HOLD IT. Gently, but very decisively, put your nose, eyes, and forehead into the water. *Look* down at the bottom of the tub. (Most books and instructors show the students going underwater in a vertical, chin-first position. Experience has proved to me that it is more comfortable to go into the water nose first. Water is less likely to go up the nostrils in this position. That's why London Bridge is a good game to play in the water. It is also why I "launch" the babies instead of dropping them or pushing them under.) Count slowly, *still holding* your breath. Exhale and bring your head out of the water. Breathe. Relax. Repeat. Be careful. Once you start to submerge your head, *do it*; don't hesitate! When bringing your head out of the water, hold your breath until your head is all the way out. The inclination is to sniff just as you start under and the instant you come up. DON'T. Try hard to open your eyes after you are submerged. Being in the dark (eyes closed) underwater is frightening and contributes to the loss-of-equilibrium feeling. (See Figure 2-9.)

Do this five times every day. If you have little ones, show them how to do it when you bathe them. If they can hold their breaths and keep their heads under for five seconds (no longer) give them a jelly bean. You can have one too if you don't get a nasal irrigation. So get busy. Go soak your head. That skill might save a life one day. **29**

"*Hurry up, Bubs,* I want to walk on the water with you," said an impatient voice. I hastened along, trying to decide if I should spoil the myth or join Bear Bryant in the book of legends. Matt was ready to get to work, and he knew that walking was necessary. It is necessary for you too. Even though it is *in* the water and not *on* it. The next skills to work on are walking, jogging, and a two-footed hop. Do them like this.

First, go to the pool. Look around and pick a fairly quiet spot in water slightly above your waist. (You can tell the depth by reading the depth markers on the deck.) Get into the water by going down the steps or ladder. Go down ladders backward. Walk back and forth slowly several times. If you feel uneasy, put one hand on the deck and lightly rest it there as you go back and forth.

Next, scrunch down shoulder deep and jog. This requires a little push off with your toes. It is not so easy and gives you a good little exercise. After that feels comfortable move on. Using both hands underwater to balance yourself, push off with both feet at the same time. Move about two feet forward with each hop. Bring your knees up high each time, and put your feet down firmly. Extend your hands sideward to balance yourself. Press on the water a little if you feel you need to. Got it? OKAY. The miracle is about to happen. You are going to combine your new skills.

To do this, you should be in water about chest deep. Station a companion with his back to the wall (so he can't move out of reach). Get about eight feet away directly opposite him. Count one, two, three; hold your breath; and put your face all the way into the water, just like you have been practicing. Start walking. HEY, what's happening? Your seat is starting to float up, and your feet are not on the bottom anymore. Keep "walking." That's right, you are moving right along. BELIEVE IT OR NOT, YOU ARE SWIMMING!!

Webster's dictionary defines swimming as moving smoothly in the water. That is what you just did. Back up and try it four more times. *Super!*

You don't look too great yet, but that's easy to fix. You have learned some important things.

30

1. How to be comfortable with your face in the water
2. How to maintain balance while walking, jogging, and hopping
3. How to float and move along without your feet on the bottom.

This plus the routine count of "one, two, three" before putting your face into the water is what the kids call the one, two, three way of learning to swim. It works. But read on—there's more to come.

Because there are many misunderstandings and misconceptions about floating, let me clarify things for you. Floating occurs when the head and lungs rest on or close to the top of the water. There are three primary ways of floating.

The Prone Float. Lie on your stomach with your face in the water, eyes looking down. Your body should be extended. Prone float is the basic body position for the crawl, the breaststroke, and the butterfly.

The Back Float. Lie on your back, face up in the water as you look straight up. Your body should be extended and your arms outstretched.

Vertical or Semivertical Floats. Put your face into water with your eyes looking almost straight ahead. Your legs should be beneath your shoulders, dangling and very relaxed. This is a deeper water float.

The secret of floating in any of these positions is to take a big breath and hold it, then put that heavy head down in the water. Many men have told me they never learned to swim because they "flunked floating." Investigation usually proves that they thought floating meant toes out of the water and head up so they could read the paper and look like the guy in the cartoons. Almost everyone floats, but at different buoyancy levels. Here is a buoyancy test I use for adults.

31

Buoyancy Test. Do this in about shoulder deep water. Stand up against the side of the pool with your arms stretched out and your chest and stomach against the side. Lean backward until your head is resting in the water, deep enough so your ears are covered. Your chest should still be against the wall. Take a *big* breath. Hold it and let go of the edge of pool. Push off gently. You should just hang there— *floating*! (See Figure 2-10a–c.)

Remember: Your lungs are your own personal built-in lifejacket. Fill them with air. Put them on top of the water, and if your head is in the water too, you will float (unless you are a *rare* specimen).

Figure 2-10a-c. *Buoyancy test. (a) Chest and arms against wall. (b) Head in water, chest up. (c) Inhale, come back easily.*

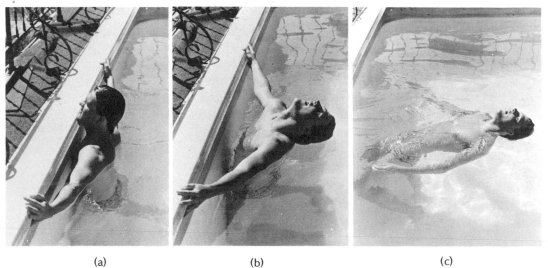

(a) (b) (c)

Holding your deeply inhaled breath keeps you floating. Exhaling will help you sink when you want to go to the bottom.

Practice skills 1, 2, and 3 on page 31 until you are comfortable with them. Then proceed, selecting the skills that are most important to you. Make your own lesson plan, always repeating each thing on your list at least five times. At the end of this section (pages 62–65) you will find the order in which I teach skills when my students have no hang-ups.

32 *Exhaling.* (Explosive breathing or rhythmic breathing)

After your face is in the water hold your breath for five counts, exhale hard on the count of six, lifting your head straight up. Look at the sky. Inhale quickly. Drop your head. Repeat. You may need to hold on to a ladder or a friend's hand as you do this because you will have a tendency to float up. *Do not wipe your eyes* or do anything except inhale when your face is out of the water. Exhale out of your nose or mouth or both, but do it *hard*!

Getting Used to Deep Water. Have a capable friend or family member go with you into the deep water. Tell the lifeguard you are going to get in and practice. Find a quiet area by a ladder. Have your friend get in and hold onto the ladder. You get in and practice putting your head in the water, while holding his hand. Try letting go. See how you stay there?

You will find that you drop a little deeper in the water after you let go, but hold still, and you will float right back up. This is called *settling*. Your position at this point will be a vertical float. You will look almost like a jellyfish. When you are comfortable in this floating position move on to *Drown-proofing* on page 54. Learn *the Rest* until it becomes automatic.

Jumping In, Turning Around

Everyone needs to know how to handle himself if he gets knocked into or falls into deep water. The most important thing is to be able to stand the initial submersion without panic. This is why you need to be able to put your head under water.

Practice this way while your friend is at the ladder with you. Pull yourself down two or three steps, let go. See how you float up? Kick your feet and press down on the water with your hands and you will almost bounce up.

Turning around is simple once you realize that your body will follow your head. Try turning around and kicking your feet to your friend.

Now it is time to try it off the deck. Stand on the side of the pool, not too close to the other wall. Jump in feet first. Start kicking your feet and turning your head as soon as you are in the water. Press on the water with your hands. Keep your face down, kick your feet, stretch your arms out, grab **33** the wall, and pull yourself up and out. The secret here is to keep your head down until you have a good grip on the wall. (This is especially important for children who push themselves away from safety if they pull their heads up too soon). Too many unpleasant reactions take place because someone less than an arm's length away from the side of a pool cannot grab the wall. Lifting the head backs you away from the wall, so keeping the head down and kicking hard helps get the outstretched hand into position for a good grab.

Treading Water

This is a necessary skill to have, but please learn *the Rest* first. It takes a great deal of energy to tread water, while doing the Rest takes just a bit more than lying in your bed. It is useful in case you need to talk to someone, and vital if you are going to learn lifesaving.

Assume a vertical position in water where you just barely touch the bottom, within reach of a ladder. Keep one hand on the ladder. Put your head back and look up, move your feet and your legs in a pedaling motion. Let go of the ladder and press your hands against water as if you were spreading flour on a breadboard or smoothing sand on the beach. Stay close to the ladder so you can hold on when you need to. It takes most beginners fifteen or twenty attempts to master this skill well enough to keep their heads up a minute or two. You should practice this skill until you can do it for about five minutes. Everyone in the family over age four can work at it. (See question 4, page 12.)

Prone Float

To teach yourself a prone float, stand in shallow water in front of a ladder or step. Rest your hands on the step that is even with the water level. Take a deep breath, hold it, and put your face into the water until your ears are in. Pick up your feet and extend them behind you in a straight position. Your arms, body, and legs should all be straight. Do not move a muscle. Hold this position for five seconds. Repeat, and this time gently lift your hands off the support. You will feel yourself settling down into the water a little; don't get excited, you'll float up in a second. Again, don't move a muscle for five seconds. *Keep your eyes open and looking down.*

34

The water really will hold you up! *Remember:* This position is the basis for all face-down strokes.

Back Float

Floating on the back is a wonderful experience for some people, but for others, it is disturbing. So, if *you* take a while to master it, don't feel silly. Not everyone learns backward skills easily because of varying degrees of balance. Also it's hard to see where you are going when you're upside down.

Your children (under age five) are frequently uneasy on their backs, and infants who usually sleep on their tummies are totally unused to being on their backs. Their balance mechanism doesn't work well upside down and neither does their vision. Adults, however, can master and enjoy the backfloat quickly.

To master the backfloat, walk a short distance backward a time or two as a warm-up and then assume the position used for the buoyancy test (see page 32). Repeat this five times or until you feel ready to move a little on your back.

Remember: Lifting either your head or your feet will send your middle down. Don't blame sinking on your "big seat." It's most likely your heavy head that's the problem. Look straight up, with your chin tucked in a little and the water right around your ears.

The American Crawl

All arm strokes are made up of four parts.

1. The catch—hand enters water.
2. The press—hand gets in position to pull.
3. The pull—the power part of the stroke that actually pulls the body through the water.
4. The recovery—the arm returns to the catch position.

Arms. The stroke for the crawl is the familiar overarm stroke that my younger students call "regular" swimming. Understanding how it works helps one to learn it, so here are some interesting facts. Approximately 80% of your power, when swimming the crawl, is provided by your arm pull. If you slap the water when putting your hand in, use a short **35** pull, or let your pulling surface (the entire arm) fail to apply pressure to the water, you are being inefficient. The most efficient crawl appears effortless. It resembles a slow motion playback. It looks strong, quiet, and beautifully streamlined. I had a little boy tell me that I looked like a "beautiful big truck" after demonstrating the crawl. For several minutes my ego suffered, then I realized what he meant. He definitely had a point. Powerful but quiet. As you practice keep that picture in mind. (See Figure 2-11a–c.)

Stand in water about chest deep or scrunch down. Extend one arm directly in front of you with your hand resting on the water in line with your shoulder. Bend your elbow and press on the water as you pull the water all the way past your hip. The elbow will be slightly bent as you lift your arm up and over the water to recover.

As you bring it over the water, straighten it so it is almost completely extended. At about the time one arm starts to recover, the other arm will start to pull. There is constant motion. One arm does not rest while the other arm pulls. Underwater your arms will work against the water, and if you concentrate on thinking about pressing backward on the water to go forward, you will almost automatically keep your elbow up (see Figure 2-11b) and your wrist straight and will pull in a sort of question mark. Your hands will actually pass under your body.

Do not cup your hands or *completely* flatten them. (See Figure 2-12a–b.) Hands should enter the water, thumb side first, in line with the shoulder.

After you have gotten the feel of the movement of the arms start walking a short distance while pulling. Do not hurry. Pull *all* the way back. Repeat.

Now it is time to put the arm movement with a prone glide. Get into the position from which you practice your glide. As soon as you are gliding nicely, begin your pull. *Remember: Long* and *strong* is what your pull should be. Pretend you are doing it in slow motion. Go as far as you can. Put your feet down and *repeat, repeat, repeat!*

The Prone Glide

Legs. The flutter kick that goes with the crawl is not difficult to learn. It is a quick fluttering of the legs as they move

Figure 2-11a-c. *American crawl. (a) Pull all the way back. (b) Keep elbows high. (c) See the air pocket by his mouth—he got a breath of air and not a mouthful of water.*

(a)

(b)

(c)

Figure 2-12a-b. *(a) No—cupped hand doesn't pull enough water. (b) Yes—flat hand has more pulling surface.*

alternately from the hips. The legs should be straight but not stiff. Think about kicking the water *up*. Feel the water on the back of your legs and on the soles of your feet. If you feel your shins or insteps slapping the water, your legs are not straight enough. So much has been said about straight legs that I have seen people so stiff and tense that movement is just about impossible. The true test of a correct kick is to kick a kickboard for awhile and see if you can get anywhere. If not, just keep at it until you master kicking. Practice makes perfect. (See Figure 2-13a–c.)

Pick a place to practice gliding where you feel secure. Some people like to glide toward a wall or beside a wall instead of toward the center of the pool. If you have a companion with you, glide off any wall to him because it is much easier to push off from the wall than from the bottom. To make this simple you must do the glide in this order. Place your back against the wall. Extend your arms in front of you. Put your face into the water. Put one foot against the wall and push off HARD. If you are properly streamlined you will probably glide 15 or 20 feet. *Remember:* Put your head in the water before pushing off or you will get a good chlorine cocktail. It helps to clasp your hands together. (See Figure 2-14a–b.) It's fun to have family contests to see who can glide the farthest. I'll bet on grandpa for this one!

Breathing for the Crawl

This is the point at which many adults give up. They either revert to a dog paddle or backstroke, or they forget swimming all together, which is terrible. When it's time to teach breathing I always feel like the doctor telling his patient, "sure you'll recover eventually, but first comes the *pain!*"

38

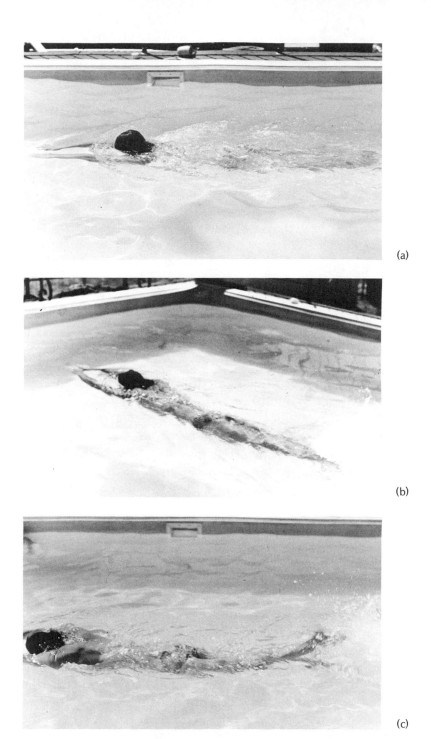

(a)

(b)

(c)

Figure 2-13a-c. *Glide. (a) Prone glide. (b) Prone glide with flutter kick. (c) Flutter kick. Note how close together his legs are.*

(a)

(b)

Figure 2-14a-b. *Glide. (a) Leaving wall with head up sinks you. (b) Head down is the correct way to glide.*

Learning to breathe easily requires practice. The only one of my students to have instant success with breathing on his crawl was a twelve-year-old child with Down's syndrome. I explained it. I demonstrated it. And then I said, "It's your turn." He did it right, over and over. The six-year-olds who have been breathing by lifting their head straight up for two or three years do almost as well. They seem to fall into the pattern naturally, almost without instruction. Perhaps the most important thing is to feel comfortable with the pull and

40

kick and to be able to exhale explosively, preferably through your nose. Then you are *ready* to learn rhythmic breathing.

Before getting into the drills keep this in mind. Pretend your head cannot move up and down. Pretend that it will move only as if it were screwed on.

There are four major reasons for difficulties with mastering breath taking. They are (1) failure to exhale, (2) lifting the head instead of rotating it, (3) short pulling, and (4) lazy legs. It is obvious that you must blow out the old air before there is room for new. Lifting the head will give you a mouth full of water instead of air. Short pulling does not give you time to exhale or to inhale, and you need the steady kick to help support the increased weight of the different head position.

The following drills will help each of the above-mentioned problems. I suggest that you do each drill several times every time you swim before trying to do them all together.

Exhaling. Hold onto the side of the pool or onto a step and put your face into the water. On the count of five, exhale hard and turn your head so you are looking directly at your shoulder. Inhale quickly and rotate your head back to center position. Repeat. Do this with sound effects. Bubble, bubble, gasp! Bubble, bubble, gasp!

Kicking and Breathing. Using a kickboard to hold onto, do the above, kicking for several laps. Keep your head submerged to the hairline. Keep your chin tucked in. Exhale hard. Turn your head to the proper side and inhale on every fifth count. Repeat.

From a prone float position, kick with your hands at your sides. Turn your head to breathe as in the previous two drills. This is very hard, and you will find out quickly why you need to kick. If you cannot master this step, go on.

Now think about your arm pull and swim without breathing for a few yards. Concentrate on a *nice, smooth, long pull.*

The next step is to get set as in Figure 2-15a–b. I recommend that you try turning your head to the left if you are right-handed and to right if you are left-handed. This is how movement education experts suggest we teach children **41** over age six. But, you may breathe on whichever side you feel most comfortable.

Start walking as you take a breath, and begin pulling with the extended arm. Each time your left hand finishes the pull, turn your head to left and inhale. *Each* time your left arm recovers put your face into the water. Exhale hard as your right arm recovers.

Okay, it's time to put it all together. Start in front of the wall. One arm ready to pull and the other to recover. Keep your ear on the pulling side in the water. (See Figure 2-15a–b.) Push off. Start pulling and kicking. You might do everything right!

Remember: Rotate your head, don't lift it. Exhale hard. Pull long, and kick steadily. You are going to make it.

Once you get it going do it over and over. Stop before you get worn-out, but remember that this is a skill that needs to be repeated hundreds of times. It eventually becomes automatic and you'll never forget it, so keep at it. When you can outswim all your eighty-year-old buddies, you'll be glad you stuck to it!

Back Sculling, or Finning

My women students love back sculling, or finning, and frequently choose to learn it first. Assume the back float position with your arms at your sides. Gently slide your hands up your body about to the waist. Extend your arms out away from your sides and push on the water as you bring your hands to your hips. Repeat. Keep your legs together and your toes pointed. If you have learned the flutter kick, you may kick slowly as you move along. This stroke is so easy and so graceful it delights everyone to see how far they go with such little effort. *Remember: Look up* and breathe regularly.

For laughs you can reverse the hand movement and move along feet first.

The Back Crawl (Backstroke)

Arms. The arms move alternately over the water, one recovering while the other pulls. To learn how to move them float on your back with your hands at your sides. Bring the

42 little finger of one hand out of the water, and keeping the

(a)

(b)

Figure 2-15a-b. *Breathing. (a) Breathing drill. Walk and pull. (b) Breathe as you finish pull.*

Figure 2-16. *Finning or sculling; three pretty finners.*

elbow straight, bring your arm in a straight line up past your ear and extend it fully, putting your little finger into the water first as far behind you as you can reach. Press the water toward your feet with your arm still straight. When your arm is about half way to your hips, bend the elbow and rotate lower half of your arm, pressing down on the water as your hand comes in close to the hips. As one arm enters the water, the other should be just about leaving it. Timing is approximate.

As you begin to swim the backstroke more and more, you will discover that you tend to roll a little. This is natural and correct, but your head should remain still. The body will

44

actually role about 45° in each direction approximately half way through each arm pull. You can feel it best by sensing the shoulder coming out of the water when the opposite arm is completing its pull.

Legs. The kick used with the backstroke is the flutter kick with toes pointed. Concentrate on kicking the water *up*. No part of the foot or leg should come out of the water. The white water is created by water being kicked *up* by the leg and feet moving rapidly just below the surface.

The best drill I know for practicing the backstroke kick is the one used by most Olympic coaches. Assume the back float position. Extend both arms overhead and clasp them together. Begin kicking. Your head must be back in the water with your ears submerged. Your chest should be high. If water runs over your head, tuck your chin in a little and lift your chest. Do not stop if you get a facefull. Rearrange yourself and keep at it. It just takes a little time.

Breathing for the backstroke is so easy that you don't have to do any drills. Breathe in on one arm pull, out on the next! (See Figure 2-17a–c.)

The Breaststroke

This is an important stroke to know because it is useful in many different circumstances. The kids insist that it's good for fooling the fish because it is so quiet. The lifeguards like it because they can see pretty well (it can be done with the head up). Many swimmers call it their rest stroke. It is a little hard to get the breaststroke organized, but stick to it. Proficiency comes suddenly.

Arms. Assume a prone float position with your arms stretched out in front of your head. Thumbs should be touching each other. Bend your elbows and press down and out on the water. Your elbows should be in line with your shoulders. Your hands will be underneath your elbows. Rotate your wrists and bring your hands together under your chest. This produces a scooping motion. The fingers will come together as if you were praying. Thrust your arms forward for the recovery and glide. *Remember:* Keep your elbows up during the pull. You should feel as if you are doing **45**

Figure 2-17a-c. *Backstroke. (a) Backstroke kicking drill. (b) One hand catches while the other finishes pull. (c) Straight-arm recovery. Arm in water is starting to bend.*

(a)

(b)

(c)

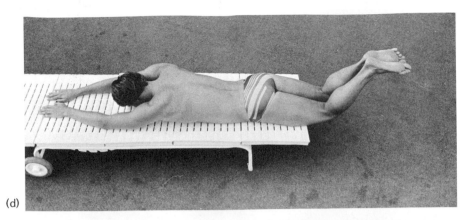

(d)

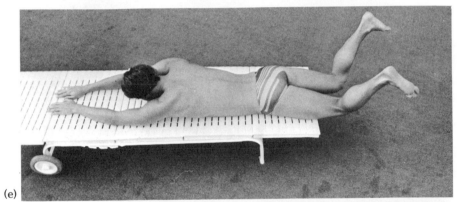

(e)

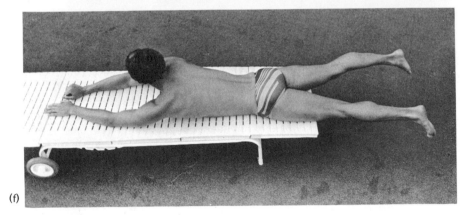

(f)

Figure 2-18a-g. *Breaststroke. (a) Arms pull down and slightly back. (b) Elbows up. Hands scoop as they come together. Head comes up to breathe. (c-g) Procedure for breast stroke.*

(a)

(b)

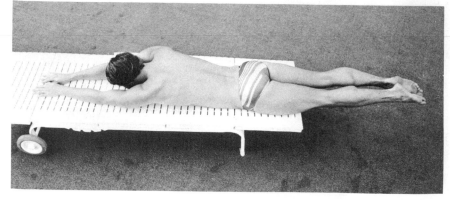

(c)

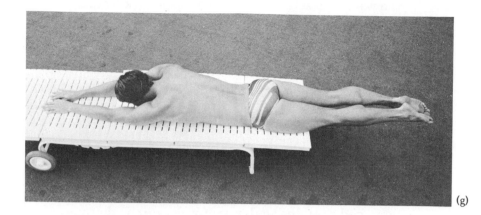

(g)

the pull in front of you. Both hands and arms should do the same thing at the same time. (See Figure 2-18a–b.) A good way to practice this stroke is to have an expert friend walk backward in the water just in front of you. You float, face down, and make your arm and hand motions match his.

Legs. The kick used for the breaststroke is called the whip kick. Lie on the water in prone float position with your legs extended. Bend your knees and bring your heels up toward your seat. Spread your knees. Thrust your feet backward, pushing on the water with the soles of your feet, and make a semicircular motion as your legs extend. Squeeze the water out from between your legs. Use your ankles and the soles of your feet to help squeeze the water. Point your toes as your feet and legs come together for the glide.

Timing. When to kick is the only part beginners find difficult. Study Figure 2-18c–g, and you will see that the kick begins when the arms are ready to start the recovery. Arms recover and legs complete the kick at the same time and glide for an instant. After trying this for several lengths of the pool, you will get the "feel" of it. There just isn't any other moment for the kick to come.

Breathing. Breathing is simple. Lift your head as you pull and inhale, drop your head and exhale as you finish the recovery and start the pull. *Remember:* Breathe every stroke. **49**

Glide at the end of each stroke. Keep part of your head out of the water. Be sure your arms and legs work *together*.

The Sidestroke

The sidestroke, like the breaststroke, is a utility stroke and is useful for many different occasions. For those of you determined not to put your face in the water, it is a good stroke.

Arms. Lie on your side with your legs together and extended. The underneath arm should be extended, and your ear should be resting on it. The upper arm should be beside your body. As the under arm pulls down, the upper arm reaches up. Both hands return to original position *and glide.*

Legs. The kick is a scissor kick and is done by bending the knees and bringing the top leg forward and the underneath leg back, as in a giant step. Straighten your legs, squeeze the water out as the legs come together, *and glide!* Arms and legs glide at same time. (See Figure 2-19a–c.)

The Butterfly

The butterfly or La Mariposa, as the Mexicans call it, is exciting. It requires strength, flexibility, and a strong sense of rhythm. It is rarely learned by anyone except the competitive swimmer. It isn't difficult; it simply is not as useful for getting around as are the others. It is essentially "freestyle doubled." Both arms move simultaneously in a wide butterfly-like motion, and both legs kick simultaneously like a dolphin's tail, and if that doesn't keep you wondering for awhile, try it. (See Figure 2-20a–c.)

Arms. Start from the prone float with both arms extended in front just outside of shoulder line, palms turned out. Pull out, down, and back, bending elbows as you pull. Slightly past your shoulders the elbows must bend, and your hands come underneath your body at about your navel. Increase the pressure of your hands at this point, straightening your elbows as you finish the pull with your hands coming out of **50** the water fully extended, past your hips. With your arms

Figure 2-19a-c. *Sidestroke. (a) Glide. (b) Pull, kick, and giggle. (c) Glide.*

(a)

(b)

(c)

fully extended and straight, bring them wide over the water and back to the point of entry.

Think about pulling your body past your hands. Get a good grip on that water and use it! The power part of the pull is the last half so don't cut it short or eliminate it. We used to joke a lot about drawing a picture of a voluptuous lady with the hands while doing the fly. You should understand that you will make an hourglass-shaped pull underwater as your hands move.

Legs. The dolphin kick is done by moving your legs up and down together at the same time. They should remain as straight as possible and should bend only slightly on the down beat.

You should feel the water on the soles of your feet, which should work as if you were wearing fins. In fact, wearing fins when you learn the butterfly is a fun thing to do. All this activity should result in a smooth undulating rhythmic motion, which reminds me of belly dancers or snake charmers.

Several years ago a nearby Catholic boy's school sent two busloads of their swim-team members to me for some coaching. It was a brand new team and the Brothers in charge knew very little about the different strokes. Teaching the dry-land drills for butterfly kicking was too much for me that day. Red-faced and holding back my laughter, I finally gave up.

Your kick should occur twice during the arm cycle—as your hands enter the water and again as your hands pass your thighs. If your pull is long and strong, the kicking is almost automatic because it is a reaction to the action of the arms. Just keep your legs together with the toes pointed, and let them follow along behind. You can just about feel where to increase the pressure and add the extra oomph to make the kicks.

Breathing. Breathe every other stroke. Lift your head barely enough to get your chin out of the water as your elbows reach maximum bend (about under your waist). Inhale as you finish the pull, and drop your head as your arms begin to recover.

52

Figure 2-20a-e. *Butterfly.*

(a)

(b)

(c)

(d)

(e)

Since I am not stressing the perfection in technique demanded in competition, I am not going to go into detail about the finer points of the strokes. The idea here is to familiarize you with them all and to let you have some fun trying to make things happen.

Drownproofing

Drownproofing, a combination of survival techniques designed to help you survive a water emergency even if you are not an expert swimmer, was developed by Fred Lanoue of Georgia Tech after World War II. Mr. Lanoue was shocked when the statistics revealed that we had lost more men during the war by drowning than by gunfire. (Even today in considerably different circumstances the highest percentage of drownings occur to young men between the ages of fifteen and thirty-four.) He experimented with some unorthodox ways of preventing drowning and worked out two principal techniques. One is called *the Rest* and the other is *the Travel.*

I consider the Rest to be the most important thing anyone can ever learn to do in the water, and long ago I started making it a part of every lesson plan for everyone from two to ninety. It can be done by virtually everyone. You can do it in pools, lakes, rivers, and even in open surf until you literally starve to death. It requires less effort than bed rest and can be done effectively even if you have been badly injured.

The Rest is done by putting your head into the water and hanging loose, as if you don't have any bones. When you feel *as if you would* like a breath, push down on the water in a sort of sculling, figure-eight movement. Exhale hard, lift your head and breathe, drop your head, and hold your breath. You should now be hanging loose again. The rest is easy to learn, and it is a skill for the family to master together. (See Figure 2-21 a–f). It could save your life:

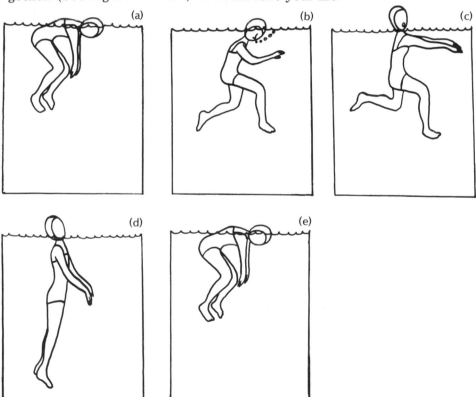

(a)　(b)　(c)

(d)　(e)

Figure 2-21a-f. *Drownproofing. In step (a), relax and hold your breath. (f) shows the travel stroke (page 56).*

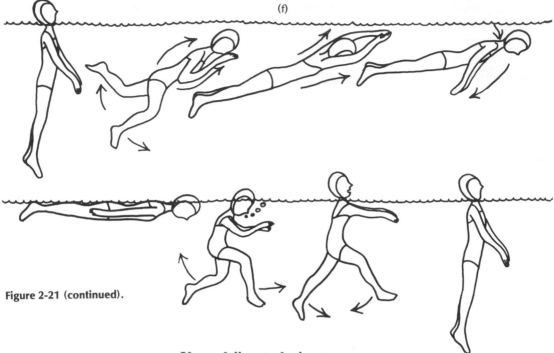

(f)

Figure 2-21 (continued).

- If you fall out of a boat
- If you fall off a pier
- If you step into a hole or unexpected deep water
- If you experience rising water due to flooding or a hurricane
- If you become tired while swimming in deep water
- In any other emergency situation in the water where you must rest and wait for rescue.

The scientific principles here are to keep the heavy head *in* the water and the built-in life jacket—the *lungs*—on top.

Practice first in shoulder-deep water. Hold on to the ladder with one hand if you feel you need support. After you feel organized and comfortable, let go. When you have mastered it there, get a friend or family member to go with you to the deep end of the pool and try it there. When you can repeat it confidently for about ten to fifteen breaths, start timing yourself. The goal for adult beginners is thirty minutes and for children, five to thirty minutes depending on their age.

At first you may have difficulty working out a breathing rhythm. The tendency is to breathe too often, which is tiring.

56

Just breathe when you feel as if you want to, and after about
five minutes, all is well.

Two of my pupils were crabbing under a nearby bridge
one day when the tide and current caught them by surprise
and first thing they knew they were being carried out to sea.
One of the boys explained the Rest to the other and promised I had said it could save their lives. A couple of hours
later, hungry and a bit frightened, the pair were rescued. It
didn't take long for the "thank-you" call!

The Travel

This unique stroke is to be done fully dressed. It is the way to
go if you must swim a long distance to save yourself. It is a
modified breaststroke that is almost effortless. The possibility could arise where you need to swim a mile or so.
Doing this in open water is much more difficult than in a
pool. The Travel is a further application of the theories that
make the Rest work, and it makes distance swimming easy.
Keep your head in the water, lungs on top, and move *tenderly*
and quietly with your arms and legs all working under the
surface of the water. Be sure to keep your head in such a
position that there are no wrinkles in your neck except when
actually lifting your head to breathe. Breathe on every other
stroke. Follow the drawings (Figure 2-21a–f) and work at this
until you can do it comfortably. Go as slowly as you can and
wear clothes over your bathing suit. Work up to a mile, which
should take the average person about an hour.

Inflatables

It's a neat trick to learn how to blow up your clothes like
balloons and use them to help you stay afloat in an emergency. Jeans, khakis, shirts, and windbreakers are especially serviceable. Clothes made of knit fabrics do not work.

If you are wearing a windbreaker, zip it up and make
certain the cuffs are buttoned. Tuck the waist into your
pants so it fits as snugly as possible. Blow into the neck
opening below your chin. Lean back and enjoy your make-do
life jacket. Long sleeved shirts can be used the same way.

Trousers also can be used. Remove them and tie the
legs together. Close the zipper. Put your head in between the
legs, so that they are like a collar. The body of pants will be **57**

on front. Blow into the waist until the trouser legs are inflated. Lean back and cross your arms on the waist to hold the air in, or, if you have a belt, tightly fasten the waist with your belt. (See Figure 2-22.)

Figure 2-22. *Inflatables. Here, John has blown his pants up like a balloon. They make a good improvised life jacket.*

Dresses, nightgowns, and skirts can serve this purpose too. Tie one end, blow into the other, and secure it the best way you can to prevent the air from escaping. You will find cotton fabrics the most satisfactory, and you may want to include a lot of them in your boating wardrobe.

Drownproofing Check List

The Rest. Vertical float in same place while awaiting rescue or regaining strength, first for five to thirty minutes, then for thirty to sixty minutes.

The Travel. Swimming one mile, dressed, for one hour, then for one hour to one hour and a half.

Tired Swimmers Carry

Accidents are frequently caused by someone in the group being too tired to return to safety. The tired swimmers carry is a necessary thing to know. The rescuer talks soothingly to the tired person instructing him to lie back on the water. Then he is told to put his hands on the rescuers shoulder's and keep his elbows straight. The rescuer swims breast-stroke. (See Figure 2-23.) He can talk to his swimmer and gently steer him back to safety. *Remember:* Always throw a rope or extend a pole if possible. Do not attempt anything unless you feel you can finish it safely.

Figure 2-23. *Tired swimmer's carry.*

How to Carry or Assist a Young Child

It is not as easy to assist a tiny tot in trouble as you think. I have been working with mothers and babies to discover the best way for them to assist their children out of deep water to safety if necessary. This is what we concluded.

Children two years old and older who have had happy experiences in the water and have practiced holding onto a rope, can be pulled ten or fifteen feet to safety. Mothers must learn to throw correctly. (See page 61.) Children can also be taught to hang on to a pole. (See page 61.)

When it is necessary for the mother to swim the child to safety, there are two possibilities. One is to have your child hold you around the neck in the front. Tell the child to look up for airplanes and then breaststroke. Even if the child leans back only slightly, it is possible to effect a pretty efficient rescue. The other method is to have the child hang on to your neck and lie on your back. This way you can swim with your head in the water, which is easier. However, with the child on your back you cannot watch the child; you can only feel him.

59

(a)

(b)

(c)

Figure 2-24a-c. *Baby assists. (a) Baby just lies on tummy. (b) Tell your child to give you a hug. (c) This is an excellent assist.*

My mothers had great individual differences in abilities, and each one decided which method worked best for her and her child. The majority chose the modified tired swimmers carry. (See Figure 2-24b.) All vowed to condition and to train themselves to handle emergency situations with more strength and confidence. Personally, I would use the assist pictured in Figure 2-24c. It supports the child completely and is comfortable for adults who can scull well.

We must strive for practical and personal applications of water safety, such as these! Find out what you can and cannot do. Borrow a friend's water-wise, water-safe child; and practice in a well-controlled situation with capable cooperative assistance available. Then teach your child how to cooperate with you. I live in a community surrounded on all sides by water. The threat of hurricanes and flooding is always with us. We *must* work at teaching families to care for each other in the event of emergency.

Elementary Rescues

Throwing a Rope or Buoy

Coil a rope and hold about half in one hand and half in the other, keeping the palm open on nonthrowing hand. Step on the end of line with the forward foot. Keeping coil or buoy parallel to your body, throw. Aim just past the swimmer's head or shoulder. Keeping your weight on back foot, lean backward slightly and pull. (See Figures 2-25a–b and 2-26a–c.)

It has been exciting to see how well young children can throw a rope and rescue family members. Six-year-olds can master the rope rescue of younger siblings. They should practice under supervision and with *water-wise* younger children. Make it important, but fun. Do not allow the children to frighten each other.

Use of a Pole

A pole, paddle, or long stick of any sort is an important piece of emergency rescue equipment. Every pier, pool, or boat should have one readily available. The pool vacuum handle, boat hook, or the dinghy's paddle all work well when pressed **61**

(b)

Figure 2-25a-b. *Throwing a buoy. (a) Be sure to step on the rope. (b) Throw over swimmer's shoulder.*

(a)

into action. The safest way to use one is to lie on your stomach with your weight well back from the edge. (Another good way is pictured in Figure 2-27.) Reach pole out to swimmer and pull slowly in.

Arm Extension

Lie down on deck. Keep body flat and well back. Reach out as far as possible and grab swimmer by wrist. Pull swimmer in from this prone position.

Suggested Goals for First Two Weeks

Paste a star by each skill when goal is achieved.

____ 1) Prone float: five to ten seconds.

____ 2) Prone glide: ten to fifteen feet.

____ 3) Back float: five to ten seconds.

____ 4) Back Sculling (finning): ten to fifteen feet.

62   When you can do this much, treat yourself to a goodie.

Figure 2-26a-c. *(a) Learning to throw the rope is fun. (b) All set. When teaching this, make it a game. (c) Child is now pulling his sister to safety.*

(a)

(b)

(c)

Figure 2-27. *When using a pole, keep your weight on your back foot.*

Suggested Goals for Second Two Weeks

_____ 1) Prone glide with crawl arm pull.

_____ 2) Prone glide with flutter kick.

_____ 3) Crawl, thirty feet.

_____ 4) Back Glide with flutter kick.

_____ 5) Back Crawl, thirty feet.

Reward Yourself!

_____ 1) Rest in deep water: five minutes.

_____ 2) Back sculling in deep water: thirty feet.

_____ 3) Crawl in deep water.

_____ 4) Jump in, turn around, return to side, and climb out.

_____ 5) Backstroke: thirty feet.

Big reward for you! Good job!

Suggested Long-Range Goals for Everyone

_____ a) To do a nice crawl for thirteen yards (no breathing).

_____ b) To do a nice crawl for twenty-five yards (breathing on the side).

64 _____ c) Scull on your back: twenty-five yards.

_____ d) Back crawl: twelve yards.

_____ e) The Rest in deep water: two to five minutes.

_____ f) Do a, b, c, d, in deep water.

Reward yourself!

_____ g) Tread water: one to ten minutes.

_____ h) Jump from side, turn, and return to side.

_____ i) Racing (shallow water) dive.

_____ j) Dive, turn around, and return to side.

_____ k) Crawl, roll over, and scull on back: five yards each.

_____ l) Jump off diving board.

_____ m) Dive off diving board.

Reward yourself!

_____ n) Travel stroke: 25 yards.

_____ o) Sidestroke: 100 to 200 yards.

_____ p) Execute elementary rescues using pole and rope.

_____ q) Emergency baby carries.

_____ r) Emergency carries with large child.

_____ s) Emergency carries with adult.

Reward again!

_____ t) Mouth to mouth resuscitation.

_____ u) Crawl for 100 to 1,000 yards.

_____ v) Backstroke for 100 to 400 yards.

_____ w) Travel: 500 to 1,650 yards.

_____ x) Rest: thirty to sixty minutes.

_____ y) Breaststroke: 200 yards or more.

For the Little People: Sing a Song of Swimming

Children really love to be sung to, and I have found that singing softly increases their enjoyment of the lesson tremendously. You can make up words as you go along, even the baby recognizes such works as "kick, kick, kick" and **65** "pull, pull, pull." The grimmest of uptight parents seem to get carried away by making up swimming-related rhymes to their favorite old nursery rhymes and songs. Here are a few as guidelines:

This is the way we kick our feet (pull our arms)
Kick our feet, kick our feet
This is the way we kick our feet
So early in the morning.

(This can be used for anything)

SING A SONG OF SWIMMING (Sixpence)*
Sing a song of swimming, kicking all the way
Sing a song of swimming; yes sir, that's the way
Pull your arms and kick your feet; close your mouth and hum,
Isn't this a dandy way to have a little fun?

SWIM ALONG (Jingle Bells)
Swim along, swim along, kicking all the way
Oh what fun it is to swim in a swimming pool today,
Oh, swim along, swim along, pulling all the way
Oh what fun it is for us to laugh and splash and play.

SEE MAMA SWIM (Three Blind Mice)
See mama swim, see mama swim
Oh what fun, oh what fun
Just close your mouth and say hum, hum
Just close your mouth and say hum, hum
Oh what fun, oh what fun!

Teaching Your Baby to Swim

Teaching your child to swim well and to be safe in the water is a long-range program that takes years to complete. The goals for particular age groups, developmental levels, and

66   *Copyright © 1975 by Maryalice F. Miner. Used with permission.

Figure 2-28. *Just close your mouth and say "hum."*

individual abilities must be carefully and objectively determined. You cannot hope to rush into an instruction program and think that your child can become competent and safe in the water in the first few years of his life. He will need supervision for a long while, but both of you will be stronger and safer if you get "in the swim" together—starting at a very tender age in an instruction program using this book. Hopefully, you will be able to swim with your child at least twice a week year-round and will be able to work with professionals specializing in instruction of the preschool child for a week or two every year.

Although I have taught many mothers with babies under six months of age, I am now recommending that babies be at least six months old before starting their aquatic experiences (unless, of course, a doctor sends them to me earlier) because by this age the nervous system is a little better developed.

Balance

Balance in the water is the basis of all satisfactory movement, just as it is on land. For the baby who cannot yet walk, how can balance be explained? It is directly related to the **67** ability of the baby to focus on a spot and direct himself to that point. The baby, when gently pushed from one person to another, will soon learn to stabilize himself.

Inflatable arm floats are a great help in developing balance. To teach a child to enjoy this swimming aid requires a very gentle, quiet approach. Let him drift along in your wake (almost vertical) as you move slowly backward. Always show him something to focus on. He can face you or you can have his *back* close to your chest. Keep the child vertical. (See Figure 2-29a–b.)

Some babies appoach this "weightless experience" with excessive movement using both legs and arms at once, turning themselves over, or ducking themselves; others will move only one arm or leg, turning themselves in circles. Either of these approaches is unsatisfactory to the baby; so sooner or later, in his efforts to avoid frustration, he solves his problem by "crawling" with the inflatable device on, thus producing an orderly dogpaddle to get where he wants to go. This helps him gain the necessary balance, and from this point on, either with or without them, it seems that rolling and turning without reason decrease rapidly. (See Figure 2-30.)

Inflatable devices should be used at the end of the lesson ONLY because if you use them after the submersions and more difficult tasks, they don't become an excuse for not going underwater. They are a little reward for doing everything else. Settle for only one submersion if you must, but add another every day or so. Practicing in the tub or backyard pool helps so much that in two or three weeks going underwater ceases to be a big deal.

The other reason for restricting the floats to after the lesson is this: If a child gets in the habit of going into the water with them already on, it is easy for him to get used to running and jumping in with little thought about how deep the water is. Use floats only after he has done his important tasks. Put them on him in the water; stay in the water close by while he swims with them on. Take the floats off, go under for a jelly bean, and then get out.

Floats are a good teaching aid. They build confidence, allow experimentation and a bit of freedom, and develop skills that carry over into many other areas. *However,* they should be used toward the end of your swim *together.* They must be kept in good repair and checked regularly for holes

68

(a)

(b)

Figure 2-29a-b. *Using inflatable arm floats. In (a), while you are moving backward, baby floats in wake.*

Figure 2-30. *Passing the baby back and forth for a short distance is good for his balance.*

or defective valves. YOU must stay within arm's reach at all times. They are NOT a substitute for a swimming *buddy,* but they serve a definite instructional purpose, which an inner tube does not. (Please do not let your little ones use inner tubes or inflatable rings until they swim well.)

Several brands of inflatable arm floats are available. The most expensive ones are worth the price, and if properly cared for, they will last two or three years. I have some that I have used six hours a day for three summers! Be sure to avoid the single compartment variety and the oversize kind that extend in the air toward the childs face.

Position

The position in which you hold a child is very important. He needs to be able to see you without turning his head, and to have close enough contact with you to be totally reassured. Remember, in holding a child, that the fear that some have to a great degree, and all have to some degree, is the fear of falling. Without mentioning it verbally, you should physically reassure the child by proper positioning so he will not feel as if he is falling.

70

The infant left on his own in the water appears to have no stability and little ability to get where he wants to go, even though he generally swims with his eyes wide open. This can be easily remedied by having the youngsters swim to their mothers who hold a brightly colored toy under the water where the baby can direct his attention and focus his eyes. This eliminates constant rolling around and turning over and helps to develop a sense of balance. (See Figure 2-31a–b.)

And On to the Pool . . .

Teaching a baby to swim is a wonderful, joyful experience. There are not many things that a mother and small child can do together that are really fun and joyous. Most babies take to water like little ducks, with abandon and pleasure. This is mostly because the prenatal influences are quite strong in a child until he is a year or so old and also because the warmth and pleasure of the companionship involved is exciting to the child.

I prefer that the infant be at least six months old, although there are some that will start earlier. At six months the baby is a "nice handful" and is fairly easy to hold comfortably, and he can smile and respond to the activity—play the games with you, so to speak. Let's pretend that you, a loving mother with a real interest in your baby, have decided to introduce him to the wonderful world of water; or perhaps you are an instructor with mothers eager to start a class. Step by step, let's get ready.

Bring along the baby's bag and a favorite goodie—teething biscuit, cookie, or the like. Bring similar things for yourself, so you can be comfortable and relaxed, and report to your lesson in a calm and happy frame of mind. You are going to re-introduce your baby to the wonderful world of water.

Let's look at our objectives:

1. To strengthen the baby's body. Just pulling a baby through the water is a resistance exercise. The pressure of the water against the body works all his muscles. **71**

(a)

(b)

Figure 2-31a-b. *Focusing. (a) Courtney is focusing on that jelly bean. (b) Jack wants to get there first!*

You'll be amazed at how different your baby will feel to you after a few weeks of swimming.

2. To develop balance and improve motor skills. That sounds like a lot for a little one, but, properly executed, the swimming lesson can help the baby master his body in surprising ways.

The mother will learn how much a baby can understand, how he can respond to a direction, and how much tolerance to the water he has. (This eliminates so much fear and distress, should the baby ever topple over in a bath or fall into a pool.)

3. To start building good safety habits.
4. Last, but not least, to enable the baby to paddle from one spot to another happily.

Lesson One

Holding your baby close to you, comfortably and casually walk into the water while talking naturally about having a good time. If the pool has steps, sit down for a few minutes where the baby can sit with his back against you and see and feel the water. Do not ask if he likes it or if he wants to get in. Do not suggest he is a big, brave boy. (See Figure 3-32a–b.)

We play many little singing games at this point including: "It's raining; it's pouring; raindrops keep falling," and so on. Children like a soft sing-songy approach, and you can compose as you go along, holding your child's hands and feet and moving them around in the water so he can feel and see the bubbles and the wiggles. Drip a little water gently on his face and head, singing and laughing a lot. Most babies will squench their eyes up, stick their tongues out, and thoroughly enjoy the experience. However, do be gentle about it.

After you both are wet and acquainted with your "big bathtub," pick your baby up again and go for a little walk around the pool, staying rather low in the water so that your shoulders are under the water; investigate things and talk about the what and where of them. When your child becomes adjusted to this, hold him out at arms' length with your hands around his chest, under his arms—not in his arm pits—and, keeping eye to eye with him, pull him through the water saying, "kick, kick, kick." (See Figure 2-33a–c.) Babies do not kick instinctively until they are released in the water, but they will learn to kick in response to the turbulence of the water around their legs and feet. Their kick ranges from a crawling-like motion to a frog kick to a one legged kick-and-drag movement. I have found that most young children who swim a lot will do all three kicks at various stages of their **73**

Figure 2-32a-b. *(a) Always carry your child or hold hands when getting in. (b) Sit down and get used to the water and the people.*

(a)

(b)

74

(a)

(b)

(c)

Figure 2-23a-c. *(a) Hold child's legs and kick them—kick, kick, kick. (b) More kick, kick, kick. (c) A-kicking we will go. Note the smiles!*

development, including no kick at all a little later after they discover they can float.

Position is important in this exercise: babies are happier if shoulder deep in the water, a bit diagonal, and looking at their mothers eye to eye. Remember that man is a vertical species, so to speak, and that your baby will swim more vertically than horizontally until he is a little better acquainted with the water. Three or four minutes of this kicking drill is quite a workout for you both. Your knees may ache from squatting, and your baby will be tired from pushing all that water out of his way; so let's go back to the steps and sit for a minute or two.

At this point you can bring in one of your child's familiar toys and play with it. Next take his hands and, pressing them against the water below the surface, say, "pull, pull, pull." (See Figure 2-34a–b.) Get back in the same position that you were in for the kicking drill and go back and forth across the pool again saying, "pull." Don't expect a real response to your request. It is really hard to get a baby to pull his hands; most of them will eventually use their hands back by the hips like little fins, but rarely do they reach out and pull until they are over a year old. Always demonstrate and encourage a long, slow pull. The frantic movements of a dog-paddle-type pull are very difficult to get rid of, once learned. Incidentally, I am opposed to teaching anyone to swim with his head out of the water (dog-paddle style) because in any emergency the head is going to go under. It is my feeling that we should prepare for this with gentle, careful submersions. So after a little work on pulling, we'll proceed to plant the seed for the next big step—the submersion. At the first lesson baby does not go under, Mommy does!

How do you feel about putting your face in the water, mother? Great, I hope, because you are going to show your baby how it is done. No funny faces, folks!

Hold your baby where he can see you. Count one, two, three; take a big breath; close your mouth; and, humming loudly, put your face into the water. Come up and say, "peek-a-boo." Smile, laugh a little, and repeat a few times.

Watching you, your baby will start to think about doing it himself. Some babies will start to imitate mother immediately. If yours is one of these, *remember:* Babies don't

Figure 2-34a-b. *(a)* Pull, pull, pull. *(b)* More pulling.

mind going underwater, and if they are put under and lifted up gently, they rarely choke. This is due to a protective device of the newborn known as a deep-dive reflex, which automatically "turns-off" the respiratory system if nose and mouth are submerged at the same time.

The trick in assuring pleasant submersions for the little ones is not to stop in the middle. If the mouth goes under, let the nose go under too. Most mothers are afraid to let this

77

Figure 2-35. *Peek-a-boo is fine, but where is my jelly bean?*

happen. Just be as quiet and at ease as you can and everything will be fine.

The first submersion is normally planned for the second
or third lesson, but a lot depends on the baby and mother.
You'll have to be the judge. Just get ready because *you* must
do it and so must your baby. It's just a question of when.

Ordinarily the first lesson ends after mama has put her
face into the water and has played peek-a-boo for her baby
once or twice. Twenty minutes of being in the water tires
children under eighteen months of age; so get out, have a
little goodie, and take your relaxed, happy baby home. Older
children can "work" for thirty minutes and play for fifteen
before becoming tired.

Lesson Two

The first part of each lesson will be a repeat of the previous
lesson. In fact, every time you get into the water with your
child, you should go through the same little routine. REPE-
TITION is one of the keys to success in any teaching situation. It is comforting to both you and your child to know
what is coming next; and, as you become more proficient in
handling your baby, you, too, will gain confidence by
repeating.

The new experience for today will come after the peek-a-boo game. After letting your baby watch you put your head underwater a few times, hold him under the arms, look him in the eye, and say, "It's your turn, one-two-three." Then, gently tip him forward so his nose and mouth go into the water simultaneously, and submerge him for a second. Come up from the water together while saying "peek-a-boo," laugh, and reach for his lollipop. Most babies will be a little surprised and, after blinking a time or two, will be ready for whatever comes next. I think it is important to stop at this point. I am sure that you had some happy giggles together and maybe sang a new song about the pretty water.

Lesson Three

Repeat lessons one and two. If the submersion goes well, repeat it, but do not do it more than three times. Be sure to tell your baby what is happening. *Remember:* one, two, three, hum is the signal to hold your breath and to get ready!

If you have shallow water, steps in the pool, or a baby pool, practice crawling. If your baby is walking, practice walking. Walking is not as easy as you would expect, and you may need to stand behind your baby and hold each of his hands with one of yours. Always hold lightly, gently, and firmly. Don't lift. Just support. Place a toy on one end of the steps, and help the baby walk to it. If there is someone with you, let your baby walk back and forth between the two of you. Use the toy as something for him to focus on. If he slips, let him go under; then pick him up gently and, laughing quietly, go find something to distract him. Keep everything low key, and baby is liable to follow your example.

Check your time. We need to introduce the arm floats in this lesson, so don't spend too long on the walking. Show the baby his "new toys." Slip one on your arm and admire it. Try it on your little one. Put the second one on and then blow them up. Play huff-n-puff or something silly. The floats should be placed very high on the arms and should be blown up all the way. If your youngster is familiar with pedaling toys, instruct him to ride his bike with his feet and pretend your fingers are the handle bars. Back up at a moderate speed. Be sure to keep your fingers limp. You should not give the child any feeling of being held up. The child should be in an almost vertical position until he gains experience. **79**

His bottom will probably float up; so reach around and gently guide it down. Almost all forward motion with the arm floats on is caused by the kick. The child's arms should stay underwater to avoid splashing himself in the face. So don't insist on pulling. As confidence grows you can let go, and you will have a swimmer kicking along in your wake. (See page 25.)

Taking short turns is helpful. Let brother and sister or friend do this too. Soon it will be fun to experiment, and you will see some interesting maneuvers. *Remember:* arm floats are *not* lifesaving devices. You should never be more than a few feet away from your "fish." For awhile it is hard for baby to get motion started on his own. It takes a little push or your wake to establish movement.

Wearing arm floats must come after at least one submersion, and you can gradually limit the time they are used.

Most children like to swim this way very much. It is interesting and necessary to note that with floats on and no one holding on, a child is as free in the water as an astronaut taking a walk in space. For some this is an uncomfortable feeling; so be patient and be happy with a little progress. One day everything will click, and you will be ecstatic.

There is no way a beginner can simply put the floats on and swim instantly. There is a technique to learning. I feel much is gained by the use of the smaller, two-compartment floats that have good safety valves. They must be checked for leaks frequently and must not be used as a substitute for a parent. Buy the good quality ones and enjoy them. (See also Balance, page 67.)

I let all the swimmers from six months to six or seven years try the arm floats. Trey was so excited when he discovered he could get around the pool without help that he called out to us, "Look, look! See this happy boy swimming by *his self!*"

It is time to take these fun things off, and play some more under the water, play some peek-a-boo and find a lollipop under the water. The child can probably handle three or four seconds under water by now. If humming does not indicate breath-holding, try explaining, "no-no" and sniff loudly. With the two-year-olds this helps, as does gently holding their noses as you tell them to hold their breath or

80

"turn nose off." Jelly beans work wonders for the children old enough to chew them because you can give a little piece after each trip underwater. Read Tricks of the Trade (page 17) for more suggestions.

That's it for this lesson. I'll wager someone is sleepy. Next lesson we will try for a real swim.

Lesson Four

By now both you and your offspring should feel at home in the water and comfortable with yourselves and the routine. In this lesson we shall proceed through all the drills and then swim. Be especially happy and easy as you prepare for the big moment. After a few good games of peek-a-boo get a bright little toy that is easily visible underwater and is exciting enough to stimulate some activity. Have someone the baby likes and trusts stand with his back against the wall. He should hold the toy under the water with his arm outstretched. You stand opposite and hold the swimmer as in Figure 2-36a–b. Give the signal, "one, two, three, hum and kick, kick, kick." Gently tip the baby forward, give him a little shove, and direct him toward the person and the toy. He will come right up to the "catcher," who should catch him with both hands *very gently*. Clap your hands and congratulate your baby. Play with the floats on for a few minutes. Repeat the "swim" and then get out. Do not let the lesson last more than forty minutes. It is too tiring and causes trouble later. Young babies may even fall asleep with the floats on. Be alert to signals of fatigue, and don't be afraid to stop in the middle of things if necessary. This is a long-range program. There is no hurry.

Lesson Five

No matter how much you are tempted, don't skip the preliminaries. By now you have discovered that some days your baby does better than others. If he is tired or cranky and doesn't have a good lesson, don't get uptight about it; this is a long process and you must not try to hurry it. In this lesson, if all has been good and happy, we shall play "pass the baby" several times. Each time give the command and allow the baby to focus on something underwater while he swims. **81**

(a)

(b)

Figure 2-36a-b. *(a) Launching Robbie. (b) Hold the toy underwater.*

Teach everyone, even the adults, to get in the habit of sight-ing on something while they swim; I encourage them to know from the very beginning where they are. I am convinced that this motor skill is important in the total development of a child. The new maneuver in this lesson is the hardest one for the mother to master. And, since it is the one that you will be doing for a couple of years whenever you swim with your baby, it is necessary to get it right.

After passing the baby back and forth a time or two, go back to the kicking and pulling position. While backing up, give the "one-two-three" count, and, without stopping your backward motion, tip the baby forward and let him go. He will kick and swim along in your wake. Sometimes he will come so fast that you will hardly be able to get out of his way. As you approach the side of the pool be sure to lift your baby out of the water before the backwash hits him in the face. After you are familiar with this maneuver try picking your your baby up after five seconds of swimming, preferably under one of his arms, and allow him to take a breath. As soon as he has taken a breath, let him go and keep moving. The first day you try this maneuver, you will usually be able to do it two or three times. (See Figure 2-37a–c.) Then, put the floats on your baby, have a short swim with him, and take him out of the pool.

Remember: (1) Tell the child what you are going to do in as few words as possible and in a rhythm. I say, "Ben, you are going to swim, swim, swim, swim, swim (maximum sub-mersion time I use), take a breath; swim, swim, swim, swim, swim; take a breath." (2) Allow adequate time for breath-taking—many brain waves must be organized. (3) Keep moving even while you are holding the child up to breathe. (4) Lift him only as high as necessary to breathe, and let go of him carefully.

Lesson Six

Lesson plans mustn't be too scheduled, and if it appears necessary to wait a day before introducing the next step, be flexible. It is better to play it by ear than to proceed with anything new before the baby is ready. After all, we are not trying to get him to swim because his friend Johnny swims but because we want to have a good time together in the water.

Figure 2-37a-c. *(a) Hold the child up to breathe. (b) Now just hold one arm.*
(c) It works with older ones, too.

(a)

(b)

(c)

In the sixth lesson I usually start teaching the babies how to fall into the pool. To do this, sit your baby on the side of the pool, and, holding him under the arms and around the ribs, rotate your wrists so that he falls forward on his tummy as you count one, two, three. After the first or second try, your baby will lean forward on his own, "dive" in, and swim to you. Thrilling, isn't it?

A word of CAUTION: Be careful not to let your baby slide in, and do not pull him in, since doing so can hurt his spine. Build the habit of tummy-and-head-first entries into the water.

Don't forget to applaud and reward the effort. I do not teach "pretty dives" to anyone until he is ready to swim in deep water and go off a diving board. Countless tragedies occur as the result of inexperienced people doing "pretty dives" into three feet of water. See Figure 2-38a–f for a fail-safe method of instructing diving that works for all age groups.

Lesson Seven

There are so many things to do in the water now, that you can't spend too long with any one. But, let me repeat, REPETITION is your friend—so is DISTRACTION—so is REWARD.

Today you are going to teach your baby how to blow bubbles. First, show him how to blow by exhaling hard on your hand; then, do it in the water. Tell your baby to blow. Take turns. Then let your baby swim while you back up, being sure that you give him a good *wake* (see page 25) to swim in, and that little by little you reduce the amount of support you give him while he breathes, by lifting his head up just enough for him to get a breath. One hand under the stomach should be sufficient by now. Always keep your hand where he can see or touch it if he wishes. Too many parents make the mistake of backing up and out of reach. You mustn't destroy the confidence and trust that you have developed, so stay close. Be sure to say, "bubble, bubble, swim, swim, swim."

You may not have time for the floats today so add some fun things in between swims and don't forget to go under-water for the lollipop or jelly beans before leaving the pool.

Figure 2-38a-f. (a) Getting set to dive in. (b) Tell the child, "Put all your weight on my arms and push." (c) "Move your arms out of the way, quickly." (d-f) Diving in.

(a)

(b)

(c)

(d)

(e)

(f)

Figure 2-39. *Blowing bubbles.*

Lesson Eight

Lessons from now on are pretty much the same. There is little that you can add except to keep encouraging your baby to lift his head to breathe. Very few babies will learn to breathe on their own until they are over two years of age, unless they are very strong. You need to add a little game we call "Turn Around, Turn Around," which is the first of the self-rescue skills. Practice this every time you swim, even though your little one may not understand it for awhile. Holding him at arms' length with his back to you, say, "one, two, three, turn around and swim to me." As you say this turn your baby around so he can see you. Do this several times, and then let him go and guide him around underwater until he is facing you; then guide him toward you. As your baby grows and understands better, hold him with his back to the wall and teach him to turn around and swim to the wall. Try placing a cookie or a lollipop on the wall, so he will want to get there. Do this with and without the floats. (See Figure 2-40a–d.)

This skill is perhaps the ultimate one. If your child can fall into the water; turn around and swim back; and learn to climb out, you will have accomplished much. However, mastering this skill is within capabilities of most children over eighteen months of age. From here on, your success will depend on keeping your baby "in the swim." Try to find a

Figure 2-40a-d. *(a) Jump in. (b) Turning around. (c) Grab the wall before picking head up. (d) Being able to climb out is essential.*

(a)

(b)

(c)

(d)

place where you can go at least twice a week and have an unhurried, unharried swim. You will feel better and so will your baby. Strength, balance, and confidence in you are wonderful things to learn so early.

Lesson Nine

I have mentioned several times that children under five years of age are not exactly ecstatic about performing maneuvers that require them to go backward. This is true on land as well as in the water, but it is important that we help them develop the ability to adjust to backward positions and activities in both environments. You can start by encouraging your baby to sleep on his back part of the time. You can fix the bathtub so he can lie on his back in a couple of inches of water and play or have a bottle. This position is also good in shallow pool areas such as around the steps. Walking and crawling backward are helpful too. When babies start to learn to swim, we need to assist them gradually so that ultimately they will learn to float and "flap, doodle, flap" (a combination of elementary backstroke and sculling). I don't remember why or how we named it that, but it is fairly graphic because the arms flap gently up and down in the water while the feet flutter gently *under* the water or even hold still. In this lesson we shall review all the things from previous lessons and then learn to "flap-doodle." (See Figure 2-41a–e.)

Put your child's head on your shoulder and his feet against the wall. Tell him to hold still. If he struggles, do something else; then, try putting him in this position again. If all is well, proceed. Put his head in your hand and move him under your chin. Tell him to look into your eyes. Hold very still. If you can count to five before he moves, great! Repeat. This time if he is still, start moving backward. When you have a good wake, let go. The child will be dragged along in his floating position beautifully. Go back to the steps, and have your child do a few up and down arm movements. Both arms do the same thing at the same time; they stay underwater and move gently from the hips to about the waist and back to the hips. Repeat, telling your child, "head on my shoulder; head in my hand; flap, doodle, flap, doodle." As you back up, carefully let go. Try to keep the child looking in

90

Figure 2-41a-e. *Flap-Doodle. (a) Start this way. (b) Head in hands, feet against wall. (c) Almost made it! (d-e) Note hand position.*

(a)

(b)

(c)

(d)

(e)

your eyes. Remind him he does not need to hold his breath but can breathe whenever he wants to. Little by little he will master these skills. A few babies and most older children learn them beautifully in time; others fight like crazy. Keep trying. Practice with the floats on. Let your child lie on the pool steps. Try it all, because when a child is in a life jacket and must be on his back he will be much safer and happier if he can tolerate being on his back.

Be sure you can do it, too!

Some Special Comments

There is a wide variance of accomplishment among young children. Be willing to accept that fact and don't compare your child with others. There are some who will watch for ten lessons and then suddenly swim on the last day, whereas others will take off immediately. This is true for infants, toddlers, and preschoolers.

Swimming for Children Is Developmental

A child goes through many phases, even some backward ones; and as he gains in strength and coordination he becomes capable of performing additional skills. It is not good to expect or demand mature stroking from the preschoolers. They need to develop safety habits, judgment, strength, and familiarity with the water. They can learn to execute a passable backstroke, a fair breaststroke, and a good crawl. However, the under-six swimmer is not consistent and is rarely acceptable by competitive standards. As long as the child is sensible and can breathe independently he should be allowed to experiment and get the "feel" of the different strokes without a lot of criticism. By the age of seven the majority of children are ready to perfect the skills. By this time hand and eye dominance have been established, and it is amazingly easy to teach them everything.

Figure 2-42a-b. *Mature stroking.*

(a)

(b)

The Two-Year-Old

Two-year-olds frequently voice their disapproval of the entire swimming scene. It really isn't the water that bothers them, it is the frustrated desire for independence and a developing ability to rationalize. A calm matter-of-fact approach, lots of distraction, and the use of most of the tricks of the trade will eventually produce a happy little swimmer. It is important to be very patient, to be content with a little progress at a time, and not to give up. The average protesting two year old in my classes is an eager convert in six to eight weeks. The protests usually stop at about the second week, progress is slow for two more weeks, and then all of a sudden you have a swimmer who doesn't want to stop! As I watch the parents and little people together, I can see the change beginning to come as soon as papa or mama relaxes and is "easy" in the water and with the child. One of the reasons for the walk-around and warm-up time at the beginning of the swim is to give the parent an opportunity to slow down and become peaceful.

The two year old is definitely a funny little fellow. First, he cries because he doesn't want to participate; then, he cries because he doesn't want to stop!

Work hard to avoid the screams, please! It is so much better if it's fun!

It may take a hundred (considered an average number) lessons to teach your preschooler to swim and another hundred to produce a safe, independent, teenager. But whatever the cost and whatever the effort, he will be grateful, and you will have peace of mind.

A checklist of skills for the young child is shown below.

Skills for the Younger Set

Paste a star by skill when goal is achieved.

Six to Eighteen Months

_____ Walks in the water.

_____ Crawls in the water.

_____ Lies happily on back in very shallow water.

_____ Kicks assisted, unassisted.

_____ Pulls assisted, unassisted (underwater pull).

_____ Hums.

_____ Puts head down and hums in response to signal.

_____ Swims approximately five feet when launched (semi-
vertically)

_____ Blows bubbles.

_____ Rides on back.

_____ Tolerates back-float position drills.

_____ Plays games.

_____ Submersion.

_____ Swims with arm floats.

Eighteen Months To Three Years
The above plus:

_____ Plays "Ring a-round the Rosie."

_____ Plays "London Bridge."

_____ Plays "Simon Says."

_____ Breathes rhythmically.

_____ Swims in wake (horizontal), breathes assisted for thirty
feet.

_____ Swims in wake (horizontal), breathes unassisted for
thirty feet.

_____ Plays "Superman" (dives).

_____ Back sculls and back floats.

_____ Somersaults.

_____ Turns around, climbs out.

_____ Jumps in, turns around, gets to wall, and gets out.

_____ Dives in, returns to side (changes direction).

_____ Retrieves objects off bottom up to three feet.

_____ Goes through hoop.

_____ Sculls (fins) on back assisted, unassisted.

_____ Out of the water recovery.

Three to Six Years
All the previously listed skills, plus:

_____ Overarm recovery with crawl.

_____ Independent breathing.

_____ The Rest (one minute to five minutes).

_____ Treading water.

_____ Backstroke (overarm recovery).

_____ Prone float.

_____ Back float.

_____ Roll over and change strokes.

_____ Proper use of kickboard.

Six Years and Over

_____ Horizontal body position should be well established.

_____ Legs should be straighter and kicking on a board should be more efficient.

_____ Breathing on the side in the crawl.

_____ Breaststroke.

_____ Surface dives (head first and feet first).

_____ Elementary rescues.

_____ Mouth-to-mouth resuscitation.

_____ Should know and practice safety rules.

_____ Use of life jackets.

_____ Distance swimming of at least 100 yards, using crawl.

_____ Ten-minute swim using any stroke or combination of strokes.

_____ The Rest (up to one hour).

Note: These are done by age simply to give an idea of what can be done under good conditions. They could be divided into stages I, II, or III. It could conceivably take five or six years for a child to master all the skills listed.

Questions Most Often Asked

Question: What should I do if my baby cries?
Answer: Try to find the cause. Burp? tired? hungry? cold? Are you uneasy? If baby doesn't stop after about five minutes

get out and try again. As the child approaches age two, we pay less attention to the cries.

Question: Why does my baby roll over, and how can I stop it?
Answer: Babies lack stability in the water. Use a toy to direct her to a spot (see Balance, page 67).

Question: What should I do if she chokes?
Answer: Gently and nonchalantly press her against your shoulder and pat her on the back, saying, "woops, too bad" or some matter-of-fact comment.

Question: When do most babies learn to breathe?
Answer: If they swim continuously (at least two or three times a week year-round), they generally breathe by age two.

Question: What is the reason for using the inflatable devices?
Answer: To improve balance and stability, to develop confidence, and—for most—to have fun. A few children can't stand to wear them, so forget it!

Question: Why doesn't my baby like to swim on his back?
Answer: Infants' balance mechanisms don't work as well as those of older children, and most babies and young children feel insecure on their backs. Try letting your baby lie on the bottom of the bathtub to play with a mobile or to have a bottle.

Question: How many lessons will it take my baby to learn to swim?
Answer: This is a difficult question because of individual reactions. Most babies "swim" by the fifth lesson, but control, breathing on their own, and good arm and leg movement take about two years to teach.

Introduction to the Diving Board

Going off the diving board is a pretty exciting thing. Children usually decide when they are ready and try out spring boards in a variety of wild and crazy ways. Sometimes my adult students get excited about going off it too and stand my hair on end with some of the stunts they attempt. When the diving board attracts you and your children, learn about it in orderly progressions. Before diving off a board, learn to jump off it. But, *do it this way: walk* to the END of the diving board. Do *not* jump off the side of the board. Do *not* have your child jump off the side of the board! It is too easy to land on the deck instead of in the water! (See Figure 2-43a.) You and your child can jump in together if you like, but try it off the side of the pool first. Hold his hand. Count that familiar one, two, three, take a deep breath, and jump. Keep your body straight when you are underwater. Kick your feet and press on the water with your free hand to hasten your trip up to the surface. Keep your head down and swim quickly to the closest side. Do not swim under the board. When your little one wants to do it alone, you may wait in the water for him. This is the safe way. Get directly in line with the end of the board. Station yourself at least a full arm's length away from the end. (See Figure 2-43b.) Have your child jump straight out. After he has left the board, kick toward him and catch his hand just after he goes under. Do not get where he can jump on top of you. Do not try to catch him in the air. Assist him to surface and have him swim to the side. If either of you cannot handle the skills involved, don't go off the board. Do not allow your child to jump off the board with *any* flotation device except for an occasional drill with your life jackets.

Figure 2-43a-b. *(a) Do not allow jumping off the side of the board. (b) Be in front of the board and far enough away to avoid being hit by the diver.*

(a)   (b)

Children who cannot handle themselves well enough to come up to the surface and to swim to the side without floats or a lot of assistance should practice their swimming before getting on the board. I have seen screaming children being dropped into the arms of waiting parents who have difficulty making it back to the side of the pool themselves. What is the point? This should be *fun*!

Skills to Master Before Diving

The closest call I have ever had in a rescue effort occurred when I went to assist a big teenager who had followed his friends off the three-meter board. I had a real struggle with him. It took all my lifesaving skills, plus a couple of nasty tricks to free myself and get him to the side. Sometime later the young man sheepishly admitted that he had *never been* swimming but had expected to be able to copy his buddies without ever having tried it. WOW!

Before diving you *must* master the following skills:

1. Swimming in deep water
2. Jumping in, in deep water
3. Turning around and returning.

To assist someone with diving, *you* must be able to:

1. Tread water, supporting someone
2. Do the tired swimmers carry or know how to assist the swimmer to the side, in case he forgets what to do.

After the jumps are going well and confidence has been built, try diving. It, too, should follow a progressive pattern. The first step is to master a pretty dive off the side of the pool into *deep* water.

Until this point is reached, all your diving experience should be limited to a shallow, racing-type dive. I feel that everyone should master this dive so well that it is automatic. Children under five years of age should not be taught a "pretty" dive because they'll do one anywhere—even into two feet of water.

The way to start working on your pretty front dive is to do the drills below. Dick Kimball, United States Olympic **99** diving coach, tells his divers, "the magic words of diving are *push off, punch in.*" Please keep his words in mind when you do the drills.

1. Kneel on the side of the pool with your toes flat on the deck so you can push off. (The water should be at least 10 feet deep.)
2. Put your head beside your knee and extend your arms out in front, pointing at the water. Clasp your hands together with the thumbs locked. Your upper arms should be against your ears.
3. Keeping your head down (top of your head should point at water) push off hard and straighten your body as it enters the water. Punch in! Practice until you are going in head first all the time. (See Figure 2-44.)
4. Diving from a standing position on the side of the pool is the next step. (See Figure 2-45.) Stand up straight with your toes curled around the edge of the pool.
5. Bend over, pointing your head at the water. Clasp your hands together also pointing at the water. Your arms should be extended and your upper arms should be as close to your ears as possible. Give a little push and fall over into the water. Straighten your body as you push and you have it! Punch in! As you do this over and over begin to work at lifting your hips as you push. This will help get a spring into the dive. When that feels good to you and everything is under control, try it off the low board. First, master a standing dive, and then you can learn how to do the approach and the hurdle, which are what makes a really nice dive possible. (See Figure 2-46.)

Forward Approach and Takeoff

Practice the approach and takeoff on the deck before getting on the board.

1. Stand up straight with your stomach pulled in and your arms at your sides.
2. Take three steps forward with your arms swinging normally.
100 3. As you begin the fourth step, swing your arms behind

Figure 2-44. *Push off—punch in, kneeling.*

Figure 2-45. *Push off—punch in, standing.*

your body; at the completion of fourth step, your arms
should be swinging forward.

4. As your arms swing forward, pull one knee up into a
   perpendicular position (hurdle). The toes are pointed **101**

Figure 2-46. *The approach and hurdle.*

straight at the board. The lifting of the arms and pushing up with the feet will lift you into the air.

Do this on the board, starting at a spot predetermined by going out to the end and marking off four steps plus about a yard for the hurdle. As your feet come down on the board after the hurdle swing both arms as if trying to pull yourself up to the sky. Leaning slightly forward *push off* and up. The board will lift you up. You will land back on it, pressing down. Then up you go, leaning into your dive. Keep your body straight; your legs and feet will rise, and your body will rotate as your feet come up to where your head was and your head drops. Stretch and reach for the water. Close your hands. Your arms should be tight against your ears. The dive should be close in to the board and the entry should be clean, with very little splash. PUNCH IN!

It is important to have a professional diving coach assist you with anything more advanced than a simple front dive. If you enjoy working on the board, get some lessons; you will progress faster and be much safer. *Note:* Learn somersaults (front and back) (see Swimmersaults," p. 125) and back dolphins, (see page 125) *in* the water before finding a diving coach!

3

How to Go Swimming Together and Enjoy It

Sometimes an eagerly awaited family outing produces misery instead of happiness. Advance planning helps prevent such disasters.

Safety tips, supplies to take with you, and games to play are all part of your fun insurance.

In case there are some stunt lovers in the family and a "ham" or two, directions for a simple water show are included in this section.

Figure 3-1. *David, Barbara, and Mike are enjoying the water together.*

Select a time when the family as a whole will be well rested and not hungry. Go with the idea of having a good time, not specifically to show off all the new skills. Some young swimmers forget everything when asked to show the family "everything you've learned in swimming lessons." When you swim in a different place be prepared for different reactions from your children. It takes a while to get used to a new environment. When I moved from one pool to another Stevie informed me, "I can't swim here, Bubs, this water is broken!"

Where to Swim?

Swim in a pool or in a properly guarded and maintained beach or lake area. If you are going on an outing and you know that you will be swimming in unguarded places, you must select your swimming spot with great care and one member of the group must be able to act as a lifeguard. *Check These Things before you swim:*

- Location of telephone. If it is a pay phone, be sure you have change!
- Is there anyone else swimming nearby? Good!
- The clarity of the water must be good.
- The bottom should be firm and not covered with trash. It should slope gently with enough shallow water for the little ones to enjoy themselves.

Do not swim in beach areas if there are big breakers or sharply sloped banks (indicating undertow or run-outs). *Do not* swim where there is seaweed, sea nettles, or indications of other plant or sea life that might be harmful.

Perhaps you plan to swim off your boat. Take the same precautions as for beach swimming, PLUS:

- Check depth with fathometer or boat hook.
- Keep radio on proper channel for emergency transmissions.
- Be certain boat is properly anchored.
- Check currents by throwing a small piece of paper into water to see how fast and in what direction it moves.
- Keep one capable guard and boatsman on board and one capable swimmer in the water. Use the buddy system.
- Take turns with the children in the water unless they are advanced swimmers.
- Swim in an area where everyone can be reached by a well-thrown ring buoy or rope.
- Stay out of the channel or other heavy trafficked areas.
- Keep clear of the propeller.
- Have a ladder for easy boarding.
- Do not allow diving in less than ten feet of water.
- Establish your limits in advance (see page 170). Appoint your guards in advance.
- *Remember:* PREVENTION IS THE KEY TO SAFETY.

108

- A standard first aid kit, plus household ammonia, butterfly adhesives, cortisone ointment, rubbing alcohol, aspirin, eye drops and meat tenderizer. See pages 111–114 for uses of these things.
- Sun screens and hats, dark glasses, and binoculars
- Beach umbrellas or tarp for shade
- Jug of water and sufficient drinks and ice
- Appropriate nourishing food that will not spoil
- Safety equipment, including ring buoy on long rope
- Whistle to signal with
- Shoes of some sort for everyone
- A change of clothes and sufficient towels
- Books, games, or sand toys to encourage quiet time
- Battery-operated or CB radio to use for weather updates.

To make your getaways easier, you can keep most of these items in your car as standard equipment.

Figure 3-2. *Take everything with you, including your own lifeguard.*

Swimming in the Surf

Going to the beach is exciting! The edge of the water where the waves lap gently on the sand is a great place for everyone to play and make sand castles. Sand sculpture is a real art, and while the younger ones create their fantasies, the family artists can build magnificent figures and designs. On some beaches contests are held and prizes are awarded for the best sculpture.

Sooner or later it is time to go into that surf and wash the sand off. The little ones will need help, and it is best to hold them in your arms until you are past the line of breakers. Watch for the white fringe of spray and feel the amount of drag as the waves come and go around your feet and legs. Excessive movement of the sand will warn you of dangerous undertow. Strong pounding of the waves with lots of flying spray indicates rough going. So take care. If you decide that conditions are favorable, the best path into the surf is by diving under the breaking wave. Then you will be where the wave is rolling gently and swimming is easy. Swim parallel to the shore. Always keep an eye on a landmark and check your position to make certain that you are not drifting away from your area. *Always* have a *buddy*! Children and inexperienced swimmers should be held by the hand and should wear their floats, and *not* inner tubes. (It is very easy for a child to slip out of an inner tube and be tumbled and lost in the surf.) Avoid pilings and piers.

Body Surfing

Body surfing is a favorite pastime of ours. To enjoy the sport, go out to where the waves begin to curl. Just as the wave crests, face the shore and glide and kick a little to get with the wave and go for a ride! If the wind is right you can get some good, safe thrills and some good laughs as you dig yourselves out of the sand. Stop before exhaustion sets in. Again, watch your landmarks. Beginners and youngsters can try their luck at body surfing but should catch their waves as they break up on the sand.

Surfboarding is another activity for the adventurer. It is easy to rent a surf board. Get an *experienced* friend or a professional to teach you how to use it and to stay with you until you know what you are doing. It is fairly dangerous, and you need to be careful on your spills to avoid being hit by the board. Good swimmers, in good shape, and in good water can have a good time. If you are not a good swimmer, if you are out of shape, or if the water is too choppy, surfboarding can be bad news.

Swimming in the River

Currents present the major problem when swimming in the river. Most currents are obvious in rivers and are easy to check. The strongest currents are found on the outside of river bends where the river becomes shallow or where it narrows. Because river water is usually murky, the depth is frequently unknown. Do not dive unless you are certain that the water is at least ten feet deep. *Note:* Depth can be checked by using a pole or a weighted rope. A snorkel and mask would help you ascertain what is underneath, but be sure all safety precautions are followed. River swimming is best when done in a marked-off, roped-in area.

Common Injuries

This section is *not* to take the place of a first aid course. It is important for everyone in the family to attend a first aid class as soon as he or she is old enough. If this is not possible, get a good book from your library and study it *together*. Have practice sessions with each other so that even the smaller children know how to stop bleeding and how to give mouth-to-mouth resuscitation. I have taught mouth-to-mouth resuscitation to five- and six-year-olds and have heard stories of children that young saving a parent's life. After one such demonstration, I asked the group what they had just learned **111** to do. A precious petite blue-eyed blond replied eagerly, "Oh, I know *that*—mouth-to-mouth *participation!*" Of course the other five-year-olds had no idea why I had such a hard time continuing the lecture. When working with the younger groups I like to present the idea of mouth-to-mouth resuscitation as "an opportunity to save a life by sharing *your* breath." This really turns the little people on, and it is easy for them to understand that this is necessary if someone appears to have fainted and is not breathing.

Head and Neck Wounds

If bleeding, apply pressure directly to the wound. Use ice for bumps, or use cool water if no ice is available. Severe head wounds and neck injuries received by diving into shallow water or by blows from boats, ski ropes, and so on, require medical attention at once. If there is any possibility of a neck or spinal injury it is best to have well-trained help in removing the injured person from the water. A backboard should be used to support his head, neck, and back. Any long board can be used. Great care is necessary and unless it is not possible to wait for professional assistance it would be safest to allow the injured person to remain in the water in a back-floating position with steady assistance to keep him level until help comes.

Prevention. *Do Not Dive Anywhere Unless The Water Is At Least 10 Feet Deep.* Young children should be taught shallow (racing) dives (see page 85), *not* "pretty dives." When they are able to handle the skills in Introduction to Diving (page 97) and have expressed interest in learning more, seek professional coaching.

Just how dangerous it can be to teach pretty dives was proven to me by a youngster who came to try out for my swimming team. She assured me she could dive in and swim twenty-five yards. She stepped up on the starting block, and before I could stop her, did a "pretty dive" straight to the bottom in four feet of water. She fractured her skull, and was lucky at that.

Abrasions

Apply a thick coat of ointment or Vaseline. After swimming, spray with antiseptic.

Figure 3-3. *What to when breathing stops.* (Poster courtesy of the American Red Cross)

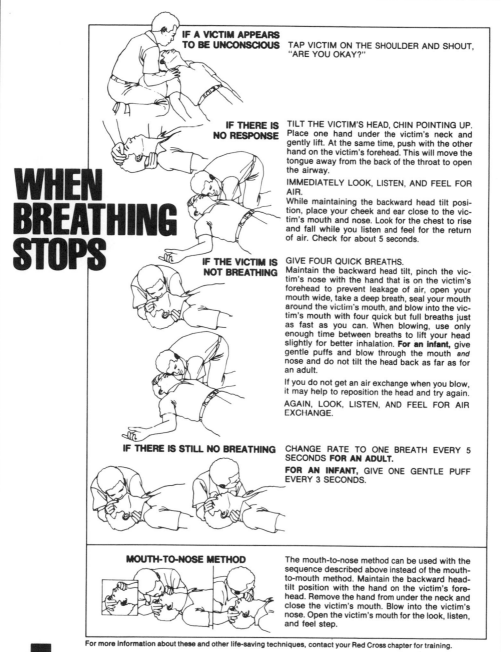

WHEN BREATHING STOPS

IF A VICTIM APPEARS TO BE UNCONSCIOUS — TAP VICTIM ON THE SHOULDER AND SHOUT, "ARE YOU OKAY?"

IF THERE IS NO RESPONSE — TILT THE VICTIM'S HEAD, CHIN POINTING UP. Place one hand under the victim's neck and gently lift. At the same time, push with the other hand on the victim's forehead. This will move the tongue away from the back of the throat to open the airway.

IMMEDIATELY LOOK, LISTEN, AND FEEL FOR AIR.

While maintaining the backward head tilt position, place your cheek and ear close to the victim's mouth and nose. Look for the chest to rise and fall while you listen and feel for the return of air. Check for about 5 seconds.

IF THE VICTIM IS NOT BREATHING — GIVE FOUR QUICK BREATHS. Maintain the backward head tilt, pinch the victim's nose with the hand that is on the victim's forehead to prevent leakage of air, open your mouth wide, take a deep breath, seal your mouth around the victim's mouth, and blow into the victim's mouth with four quick but full breaths just as fast as you can. When blowing, use only enough time between breaths to lift your head slightly for better inhalation. **For an infant,** give gentle puffs and blow through the mouth *and* nose and do not tilt the head back as far as for an adult.

If you do not get an air exchange when you blow, it may help to reposition the head and try again.

AGAIN, LOOK, LISTEN, AND FEEL FOR AIR EXCHANGE.

IF THERE IS STILL NO BREATHING — CHANGE RATE TO ONE BREATH EVERY 5 SECONDS **FOR AN ADULT.**

FOR AN INFANT, GIVE ONE GENTLE PUFF EVERY 3 SECONDS.

MOUTH-TO-NOSE METHOD — The mouth-to-nose method can be used with the sequence described above instead of the mouth-to-mouth method. Maintain the backward head-tilt position with the hand on the victim's forehead. Remove the hand from under the neck and close the victim's mouth. Blow into the victim's nose. Open the victim's mouth for the look, listen, and feel step.

For more information about these and other life-saving techniques, contact your Red Cross chapter for training.

AMERICAN RED CROSS   ARTIFICIAL RESPIRATION

Poster 1002-A
Rev. April 1978

Prevention. Don't run!

Sea Nettle Stings

Remove tentacles and all pieces of the animal with whatever you can find, including seaweed or sand. Wash with baking soda and water, fresh water, or household ammonia. Meat tenderizer is considered an excellent treatment by Gulf Coast fishermen who always keep it available. It contains an enzyme that destroys the toxic proteins.

Do not use iodine, merthiolate, or salt water. See a doctor for severe cases. Medical attention is vital for man-of-war or sea wasp stings.

Prevention. *Be Alert.* Check areas before *swimming.*

Nose Bleeds

Nose bleeds are fairly common around pool and beach areas because children bump each other or swim into things. Simply have child sit quietly in your lap and pinch his nose gently for two or three minutes, or press a finger firmly against the upper lip where it joins the nose. Keep the child erect; do not have him lie down.

Prevention. KEEP ROUGH PLAY UNDER CONTROL.

Slit Chins

Another frequent injury for the younger set is the slit chin that comes from hitting the chin on edge of the pool. The wound is nasty looking because although there is a lot of flesh in the area, the bone is usually visible. Dry the wound carefully, pull the two sides of the cut neatly together, apply butterfly adhesives, and spray with a nongreasy antiseptic. Usually stitches can be avoided, but careful attention is essential. If you don't have butterfly adhesives and don't know how to make them, it is best to seek medical advice.

Prevention. DO NOT ALLOW BACKWARD JUMPING
114 OFF DECK. (See Figure 3-4a–b.)

(a)　　　　　　　　　　　(b)

Figure 3-4a-b. *Preventing slit chins. (a) No—do not allow backwards jumping off the deck. (b) Yes—always dive from a forward position.*

Family Fun and Games

"Ring-a-round the Rosie"

In shallow water hold hands and hop slowly around. (Hold the too-short ones on your arm). Sing "ring-a-round the Rosie, Pocketfull of Posie, one, two, three, put your chin in the water." Stop while everyone puts his chin in. Repeat,

Figure 3-5. *"Ring Around the Rosie," family style.*

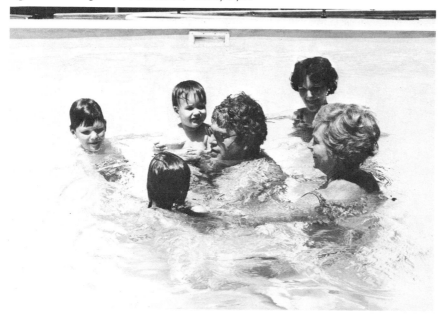

each time substituting one ear, the other ear, both ears, gradually getting up to "one, two, three, take a breath and all put your heads in the water."

I do not tell everyone to "all fall down" until I know everyone in the group can handle it happily and safely.

"London Bridge"

Have one member of the group stand by the side of the pool in shallow water, scrunched down so that he is shoulder deep. Have him make the bridge by extending his arm and holding on to the side of the pool, allowing sufficient headroom between the arm and water. Have another member stand next to him to assist the players and head them back to their place in line. Sing "London Bridge is falling down" as players walk under the bridge. Some will put their faces in; others will not. Do not comment on those who don't; clap and cheer for those who do. After everyone has been through once drop the bridge a little lower. Do this until the arm is in the water. Be sure that the adult family members have their turns. If you have a baby or toddler let him go too—in your arms or however you can work it out. Keep the line moving; keep singing and laughing and clapping. If someone balks,

Figure 3-6. *Mike just swam under a long London Bridge.*

lift the bridge a little bit and tell him to sneak under. He'll come around if you don't make too big a deal out of it. Watch the limbo artists master this! When everyone can do it, make a long bridge. Have the person at the end of the line swim through and rejoin the bridge at the other end.

Treasure Hunts

Treasure hunts can vary in numerous ways, ranging from hunts for jelly beans to pennies. One of our favorites is hunting for brightly colored plastic easter eggs. Fill all but one with something heavy to weight them enough so they'll sink about a foot or two beneath the surface. In the remaining egg—or two, depending on how large the group— put the treasure. Make sure in advance that it will sink too. Have the players close their eyes while you hide the eggs. Place them in safe, accessible spots in the proper depth water for your players and then say, "go."

Another favorite is hunting for plastic string beads and bracelets. This is a good treasure hunt to use at birthday parties.

Legs

Players make a line and spread their legs apart. The swimmer at the back of the line goes under water and swims through all the legs to the front of the line. Then, it is the next swimmer's turn.

Simon Says

This is another adaptation of an old game. One player is Simon. He stands in front of the group, which should be seated on the steps or standing in shallow water. He tells them, "Simon says float on your back" or "Simon says blow a bubble" or whatever skills he thinks are appropriate. Everyone does it together. Since the purpose is participation, there are no "outs," but after the original Simon gives five "orders," he appoints the swimmer that he thinks did the best to take his place. Each child should have his turn at being Simon.

117

Building Pyramids

Our family always loved to do this. Be sure to observe the safety rules and work in the middle of the pool when there are no other swimmers nearby. The adults can get the younger children set up and then go underwater and lift them to their shoulders. Learn to fall away from each other if it doesn't work. (See Figure 3-7a–c.)

(a)

(b)

Figure 3-7a-c. *Building pyramids.*

(c)

Let's Pretend

This is a thinking game. The purpose is to solve a problem thought up by the leader, who must be mature and aware of

118

the group's capabilities. Some typical problems would be:

- Someone pushed you into the pool. What would you do? (Turn around, go back, and climb out.)
- Your money fell to the bottom in two feet (four feet, five feet) of water. (Use a surface dive.)
- You dropped your fishing pole off a pier. (Let it go.)
- You suddenly stepped into deep water. (Put your head down, turn around, go back).
- You are swimming across the pool and get tired. (Stop and do the Rest, then continue).
- Your boat sank. (Practice this with and without life jackets, provided everyone is ready).

Start with the older family members and try to let everyone work out the solution. If anyone appears to be attempting an unsafe or unsatisfactory solution watch him carefully. Stop at the first sign of distress. (Don't forget that head shaking and looking "stuck" are signs of difficulty. Demonstrate a better way. Have everyone practice skills if necessary. Don't be afraid to encourage everyone to try, but be alert and *be available.*

Water Baseball

Use weighted frisbies or similar plastic toys as the bases and home plate. Use Ping-Pong paddles and balls or a lightweight plastic bat and ball. Use regular rules. Play in shallow water, but encourage players to swim. If one child cannot swim well enough, let an older sister or brother carry him piggyback.

Water Polo

When everyone swims well and treads water comfortably, water polo is a tough and exciting game to play.

You will need a volleyball and two goals, one on each side of the deep part of the pool. Goals can be designated areas, marked off with towels on the deck, and should be about six feet wide and long.

Divide your group into two teams. Assign one person from each team to be goalie. His job is to tread water in front **119** of the goal area and deflect any ball before a member of the opposite team throws it into the goal area. (Normally, a net is used, but for informal play, consider the concrete the goal.)

The two teams take positions in the water defending their goals (facing each other). The referee on deck throws the ball into the center and who ever makes the catch proceeds to move the ball, as in basketball, across the pool to the opposite goal. He can swim with the ball in between his arms or under his chin with his head up. He can pass. Opposing team members can steal the ball or intercept a pass. When the one with possession feels he can get the ball into the goal area he should throw. If the goalie cannot hit the ball and send it away before it touches the side of pool or deck within the goal area, the advancing team gets a point.

For family water polo it is advisable to limit the game to five minutes. Players should not be allowed to touch each other or to hold each other underwater.

It takes skill to "dribble" the ball, to tread water, and to swim with the head out of the water, so practice in between games. Play informally, family against family, at the neighborhood pool until the game is going well and then learn the bona fide rules and make up some appropriate teams.

Water polo is an Olympic sport. Some high schools and swim clubs have teams. Swim teams use it as a gimmick to break the monotony of training schedules, and it is a different kind of a family water game. The standard rules must be adapted to suit the ages and abilities of family members. With a little caution it can provide outstanding activity for an otherwise quiet time at your pool.

"Favorite Ball"

This is an indvidual game, not a team game. Outline a playing area and a goal area. Designate one large or two small goalies. Their job is to keep the ball from touching the water in the goal area. Everyone else takes positions in the pool. The goalie throws the ball into the pool and everyone tries to get it and throw it past the goalie to score a point. If the goalie intercepts a pass, he gets a point. Players can steal the ball from each other and can intercept passes, but they cannot touch each other. Parents and older players can hold younger ones so they can play too. At the end of five minutes

Figure 3-8. *Our favorite ball game.*

the person with the most points is the winner. Change goalies and play again. Families really like this game. It is perfect for a home pool with steps at one end. Use a partially deflated volley ball. Do not allow excessive roughness.

Relays

Relays are always fun. They should be set up with teams as nearly equal in number and skill as possible to keep things fun and exciting. The relays listed below are all "shuttle" relays where teams are split and half the members of each team are at opposite sides or ends of the distance to be covered. The rule for all these relays requires the incoming swimmer to touch a hand or foot of the next participant. This eliminates "fudging" (cheating). I told a little girl she "fudged" in a relay, and she smiled sweetly and replied, "Thank you!"

Blow the Ball. Walk or swim. Relay members blow Ping-Pong balls across the pool to their team mates. Hands must be kept behind backs.

Tee-Shirt. (Swim or walk.) Use a large tee-shirt so mom and dad don't strangle. Relay members swim or walk to the team member who is wearing the shirt, remove the shirt, put **121**

Figure 3-9. *Tee shirt relay. Pull shirt over heads, pass shirt from one member of team to another.*

it on next team member. This gets hysterically funny. (See Figure 3-9.)

Twins Racing. This relay is done in pairs. Two members of each team hold hands and swim together to two team mates who repeat. This is fun with father-mother and brother-sister combinations.

Drag Racing. This relay is also done in pairs. The larger person assumes a prone float. The smaller person grabs his ankle and also assumes a prone float. The first person pulls, and the one in back kicks. Arms and legs must stay straight.

122

and the one in back kicks. Arms and legs must stay straight. You can also try a piggyback realy for very small children who can't hold onto another's ankles. (See Figure 3-10a–b.)

Figure 3-10a-b. *Piggyback relay. (a) Three teams run or swim in. (b) Team members run or swim back.*

(a)

(b)

Umbrella Race. Each team has one umbrella, which is opened. Team members alternate swimming on their backs or sides with the open umbrella. The first team to finish and close their umbrella wins.

NOTE: Jelly beans or some goodie for winning team members adds to the fun.

Games Not to Play

See Who Can Stay Underwater the Longest

Please, I beg you, do NOT play this game. Those of us who train swimmers are familiar with the tragic consequences of staying underwater for a long time, and we do everything we can to discourage contests of this sort. Do not allow anyone you know to do it. DO NOT suggest this game as a means to teach a child to go underwater or to float. Stop anyone you see or hear getting ready to do it, or alert the lifeguard at once. This is why: When the brain does not receive enough oxygen things "gray out." The swimmer is not unconscious, but he is out of touch with reality. He continues to move although his coordination is poor. The mechanism that triggers breathing does not work, and suddenly the lungs rupture or the swimmer dies from self-suffocation. Only a lifeguard with a great deal of experience can recognize the signs before it is too late.

See Who Can Swim the Farthest

Obviously, this is foolhardy. Dares of any sort or games that have a swimmer doing things beyond his capabilities *must* be avoided.

Water Show

Stunts

These stunts are adapted from water ballet stunts. It is quite possible for a family with big age gaps to put together a water show for other family members or for a party. Mother and daughters can select some music, choreograph a routine, and make costumes. Or the girls and boys can do the swimming, while mom provides the direction and does the sewing. Dad and the boys can do a clown act; mom and dad, a duet routine.

Almost everyone in the family can learn these simple stunts and combine them with back finning and the breaststroke to make an effective performance. If you enjoy it, look for an existing team and participate in a big way. Synchron-ized swimming (the real name) is also an Olympic sport.

Surface Dives

Learn surface dives by swimming breaststroke. As you begin a pull, drop your head and bring your hips up hard; and as you go toward the bottom, straighten your legs and point your toes. You should be vertical, head down, and in position to do a hand stand or to swim down to the bottom. (See Figure 3-11.)

Figure 3-11. *Surface dive.*

Back Dolphins

To do a back dolphin, first, float on your back. Then, arch your back and put your head all the way back. Stretch your arms overhead and push up on water. This will pull you around in a perfect circle right back to your original position. Do not twist your body, turn your head, or cave in, in the middle. Keep your legs together and point your toes. Very pretty! Exhale slowly as you go around. (See Figure 3-12.)

"Swimmersaults"

Recently at class, somersaults became "swimmersaults" at the request of an original six year old. People of all ages enjoy these if they can hold their breath well. The bottom **125**

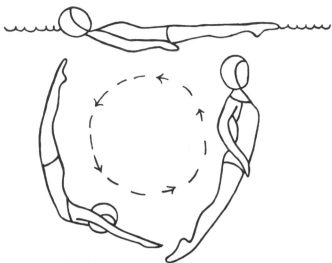

Figure 3-12. *Back dolphin.*

step of the pool is the best place to learn these. Stand facing the water. Push off hard into a tuck position, bringing your head around toward your knees. Use your arms to push the water up. This should spin you right over. Even three-year-olds can do two or three somersaults without surfacing.

Oysters

"Oysters" are accomplished from a back float. Stretch your arms overhead by moving them out to the sides. When they reach full extension and you are in a straight position, bring your head and feet out of the water, and touch your hands to your feet. You will be in a pike position and will sink quickly. BUMP!! (See Figure 3-13.)

Marching

Scull on back and alternately slide one foot up the other leg to knee in time to music. Up, one, two; down, three, four; other leg up, one, two; down, three, four. Keep your body straight and scull with your hands close to your hips.

Ballet Leg

"Ballet leg" is a difficult stunt that results in lots of giggles, if **126** nothing else. Try getting Father to learn! The boys love to

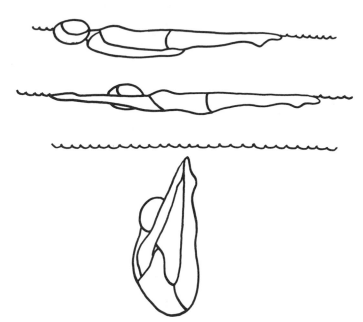

Figure 3-13. *Oyster.*

clown with this, so if they mimic, recruit them to do a funny act.

Lie on your back and scull. Bend your knee as in marching, then straighten your leg to a vertical position. Keep your toes pointed. Hold two counts, bend your knee, and return your foot to the original position by sliding it along your leg. Leg up, one, two; straighten, three, four; leg down, five, six. GLUB! GLUB!

Shark

Lie on your side just under surface. Bend your upper arm over the side of your head. Arch your body and pull around in a circle by sculling with the arm that is under your body. This can be done with a graceful rounded arm position or with a sharply angled one. EASY! (See Figure 3-14.)

Water Wheel

Water wheel is a deep water stunt. Two or more swimmers float on their backs and each puts his or her feet under the other's chin. The first swimmer executes back dolphin; the others follow. If all swimmers keep their backs arched and **127**

Figure 3-14. *Shark.*

pull around quickly, this stunt is successful. If anyone goes limp or twists, it won't work. It's *hard* but worth it.

Patterns

This stunt can be done in lines or in pairs. Floating on your backs, form a circle with your toes touching in the center. Spread your legs and close them. (The circle will change size.) Kick to make a pretty splash. Oyster together and the circle disappears: Swim underwater into position for the next stunt.

Strokes

Strokes are the basis of your routines. Pick a stroke that suits your music. If you are all beginners, sometimes its better to pick the music to fit what you all can do.

Crawl. For water show routines do the crawl with your head up and eyes straight ahead. Your feet will be quite deep in the water, so use a flutter kick underwater or a combination flutter-frog. Many variations are possible such as the wave-stroke (see Figures 3-15c and 3-16g), hesitation stroke, salute stroke, splash stroke, or one we always call the hoochie-kootchie. All can be turned over and done on your **128** back. (See Figure 3-16g.)

Breaststroke. In water routines the breaststroke is very necessary to equalize patterns when tall and short swim together. It is easy to keep heads in a row. The breaststroke can be done all underwater or with a rolling, short recovery out of the water. (See Figure 2-18a–g.)

Waltz Crawl. This stroke is beautiful and not too complicated if everyone will remember to roll on the arm in the water on the third beat. Use an overhand crawl, and count it: one, two, three, roll (right, left, right, roll to the right). Find music with a heavy waltz beat, such as "Blue Danube" or "Tales From the Vienna Woods."

Overarm Sidestroke. This stroke is best done in pairs, one partner swimming on the left side and the other on the right. Do a side stroke, but bring the top arm out of the water on the recovery. It is effective for partners to touch fingertips together while recovering. This is a good stroke to be used with the shark.

A Sample Water Show

Remember the purpose of this routine (pages 129–131) is not to produce a perfect piece but to have fun creating and doing something together. After you have put this together, try an original. Soon you will be ready to strive for bigger and better shows.

Water Show Routine

Music: "Blue Hawaii" (*Note*: This particular type of music was selected because it has a gentle beat and because swimmers do not have to stay exactly with the music. Other selections of similar flowing style can be substituted.)
Time: Approximately three and a half minutes.
Costumes: Brightly colored suits. Swimmers can wear leis or put flowers on their kickboards or in the pool.
Equipment: A kickboard for each swimmer, Tiki torches for poolside if it is an afterdark performance. Record player or tape recorder.

(a)

Figure 3-15a-d. *(a) Six to sixty, water ballet is fun. (b) Learning to march. (c) Wave stroke (walking). (d) Another pretty formation for water ballet.*

(b)

(c)

(d)

Number of Swimmers: Two to six.

Size of Pool: This was choreographed in our 16 × 32-foot pool with steps at one end. Adapt it by adding or subtracting strokes.

Strokes Used: Backstroke, Modified breaststroke, Overarm sidestroke, Wavestroke, Modified backstroke.

Stunts Used: Shark, Surface dive, Bent knee, Marching, Oyster.

Patterns Used: Circle into star.

Special Effects: Twirling around in circle, using thumbs to splash water. Leaping out of water in a circle, holding hands.

Positions for Entrance: Half at one end of pool, half at steps on other.

As music begins swimmers walk gracefully into water holding kickboards. Swimmers on far end swing legs over the side and ease in. All kick to the center and kick around in one complete circle. Swimmers peel off and form a line facing steps. Kickboards are placed on corners. (See Figure 3-16a–b.)

Leaning backward slowly, seven backstrokes are executed. Start with right hand. Watch each other by rolling your eyes, do not turn your head. Keep arms moving with each other. (See Figure 3-16c–d.)

If there are two or four swimmers face each other; if there are three, swim in a V formation. Do four overarm sidestrokes and the shark (eight counts). (See Figure 3-16e.) Do one modified breaststroke to the steps.

Form one long line and wavestroke on right arm only. (See Figure 3-16f–g.) When first swimmer is two-thirds of way down the pool do one-half shark (four counts).

Leave side on backs. Scull, allowing four counts, do bent knee march. (See Figure 3-16h.)

Swimmers will pass in between each other. When heads touch wall, put feet down and gently leave using one breaststroke. Surface dive. Swim to side.

Leave side on back. Do modified backstroke until swimmers are in line. Scull into circle, toes touching (four counts). (See Figure 3-16i–j.)

Separate legs. (See Figure 3-16k.) Keep toes touching. Close legs (four counts).

Kick four counts (Figure 3-16l). Oyster (Figure 3-16m). Swim underwater, hold hands. Leap into air, releasing hands as they are raised overhead (Figure 3-16n). *Yea!!*

131

Figure 3-16a-n. *"Blue Hawaii" water show. (a) Entrance. (b) Circle kicking. (c) Back-stroke. (d) Backstroke. (e) Shark. (f) Twirl in circles, thumbs down, make lots of spray. (g) Wave stroke. (h) Bent-knee marching. (i) Modified backstroke. (j) Circle—legs together. (k) Star—legs apart. (l) Kick out. (m) Oyster. (n) Jump way up!*

(a)

(b)

(c)

(d)

(e)

(f)

(g)

(h)

(i)

(j)

(k)

(l)

(m)

(n)

4

Building a Better Body

How to plan an exercise program to benefit *you* is outlined in this section. Questions are answered on the care of hair, skin, and eyes, ears, and nose. Water exercises for those not wanting to get their hair wet are explained. (Don't look now, but I think it's a trick to get some of you *in* the water).

If you have a child interested in competitive swimming, you will find some hints and opinions about selecting a team for him.

Swimming is a better overall exercise than any other sport (except cross-country skiing) because nearly every muscle in the body has to work as you pull and kick against the resistance of the water. It puts enough stress on the cardiovascular system to improve its efficiency; and, yet for some of us, it is more pleasant and more satisfying than running, which is the most popular of the fitness sports. Personally, swimming is my sport, and try as I may to be a runner, I prefer the pool. I like being supported by the water and that wonderful feeling of stretching as I pull along so smoothly through my quiet, peaceful world. The quick inhalation of blessed oxygen becomes more and more intoxicating as my swim progresses.

My friends ask, "Doesn't it get boring to just get in and do lap after lap?" For me it is the only time of the day for uninterrupted thought so I relish the monotony. My best plans are made while I swim. I used to tell my racers to practice their multiplication tables or their math formulas during warm-up time. But, I think about everything as I chug along.

Recently I have found myself concentrating on ways to convince others how great it feels to be a swimmer. Just think about this, ladies—with one activity you can build a better bustline, help a sagging chin, stop drooping upper arms, and do spectacular things for your legs and hips. You can also stop huffing and puffing.

As for you men, just think about those trim and superbly proportioned physiques of our Olympic swimmers. If that doesn't spur you on to try swimming, maybe this will. A friend of ours who has been swimming a mile a day for years came up to me on the street and told me he had recently suffered a heart attack. He laughed at my surprise and explained that his doctor had told him that he was   **139** fortunate because his swimming had kept him in such good shape that surgery was not necessary. He had made a quick recovery and was back working out.

For years it has saddened me to see the poor physical condition of the mothers whose children I teach. Thank goodness the current trends for fitness are convincing more and more women, as well as men, that there is more to being in shape than just SHAPE.

It's an experience to work up a sweat while swimming—and one I'd like you to share with me. Try it. You'll feel refreshed, strong, powerful, and relaxed. What more can I say? GET IN THE SWIM!

Planning Your Exercise Program

Now that you are eager to be a swimmer, go to your doctor for a checkup and a stress test. Armed with his blessing and your own desire for self-improvement, head for the swimming pool. Allow a couple of minutes for walking and jogging in the water. Then do two or three minutes of the exercises found in the section of Aquaticalisthenics (page 143). It is necessary for the swimmer to warm up, just as it is for runners and cyclists. Don't skip it. The few times I have tried to save time by eliminating the warm-up, my body has complained loudly. When you feel loose and ready, go ahead and gradually start building strength by following the programs that follow.

The whole family (those over eight) can work on these programs together, which makes exercising more exciting.

The crawl is the best stroke to use for a fitness program. If you prefer to use another stroke, use the same stroke for the entire workout and recognize that you will probably have to swim for a longer period of time to get your pulse rate up to the training rate. The breaststroke, sidestroke, or backstroke would be satisfactory. The butterfly is not recommended.

Your *heart* is the controlling factor in the organization of your·workout. It is a wonderful, hardworking, muscular pump. Our ultimate goal is to strengthen the heart muscle so

140 it will have to pump less often to distribute the blood to all parts of the body. This is done by putting stress on the muscle for increasingly long periods of time. Training pulse rates for all ages have been established, and research has proved that this rate must be sustained for at least twenty minutes for maximum benefit to be obtained. You will discover as you progress that you will have to swim faster or further to keep your pulse rate up for the desired period of time. Whenever you start to get weary, think about this interesting fact: research indicates that vigorous swimming counteracts the effects of old age.

To take your pulse, put the third and fourth fingers up against either side of your adam's apple and press firmly. Move your fingers around until you feel a good pulse. You can count it on your wrist or directly on your heart, if you wish. Do not use your index finger or your thumb.

The First Week

Plan to swim for fifteen minutes, on three nonconsecutive days. Record your pulse rate before starting. Swim seven and a half minutes. Check it again. If it is too high, slow down or walk for awhile, and remember to start at a slower pace the next time. If your pulse rate was too low, speed up. Be aware of how you feel, and *remember that the time spent swimming is more important than the distance covered.*

Check your pulse rate again immediately when your fifteen minutes are up. Rest one minute. Check again. It will drop dramatically between thirty and forty-five seconds after you stop swimming. It should be back to normal within five minutes. If it is not, slow your program down the next time.

As you become familiar with how your body works and feels, you will be able to guess your pulse rate within a beat or two during your exercise period.

The Second Week

Extend your swim to twenty minutes. Take your pulse halfway through and at the finish the same as last week.

The Third Week

If all is well and you are keeping your pulse rate within the recommended range, lengthen your swim to thirty minutes. The distance will change, just be sure to keep your pulse rate within the training range shown in the table below.

Training Pulse Rates

Age	Average	Maximum
Under 25	136–166	195
25–35	130–158	185
35–45	123–149	175
45–55	116–140	165
55–65	109–132	155
65–75	102–123	145

If you have chest pains, stop immediately and consult your doctor. Be sensible; be logical. Be smart about your heart!

Equipment

Be sure to wear a comfortable suit to work out in. Most department stores stock lightweight nylon swim suits for both men and women. Women should buy a suit that stretches enough so that it doesn't chafe or bind under the arms or around the neck. Bikinis are out for this activity, as are suits with ruffles, fancy skirts, or trimming. Fortunately, the colorful one-piece suit is very stylish as well as practical.

Suits for men should be lightweight and not bulky. The nylon athletic boxer is a good choice, if you don't care to buy a racing suit. Several companies make a modified racing suit that is comfortable for the serious swimmer.

Reward yourself somewhere along the line with a good warm-up suit. You can wear it on many occasions, and it is a luxury to put on when you finish.

If your pool does not have a big pace clock, buy an inexpensive waterproof watch with a second hand.

Masks and Fins

If you have problems learning breath control but enjoy swimming otherwise, I see nothing wrong with using a face mask and snorkel. (See page 158.)

These exercises are stretching and warm-up exercises that can be done for a five-minute period before your conditioning swim. If you are a nonswimmer and want to get used to the water and get in shape at the same time, put together a combination that will keep you moving at a steady pace for twenty minutes. As always, start slowly and build up gradually.

- Get in and walk in shallow water for two to three minutes.
- Make ten circles with your arms.
- Make ten circles with your shoulders (bring them high and stretch way back).
- Make ten circles with your elbows (again stretching).
- Make ten circles with your hands.
- Make 5 circles with head (pretend you are drawing them with your chin).

Jog. Get in shoulder-deep water and jog back and forth across pool slowly for 1 minute.

Jumping Jacks. Place your hands on your hips and do the leg motions of jumping jacks.

Lunge. With your hands and arms outstretched, one leg in front and one in back, jump up and change the position of your legs.

Torso-stretching with Kickboard. Grasp the kickboard in both hands. Keeping your elbows straight, draw circles with board. Do ten. (See Figure 4-1.)

Figure 4-1. *Kicking with a board builds endurance, trims stomach and legs.*

Figure 4-2a-c. *(a) Water press works chest muscles and triceps. (b) Walking the wall is a great flexibility exercise. (c) Rowing is fantastic for general conditioning if you do it fast.*

(a)

(b)

(c)

Water Press. Use a kickboard in each hand for this. See Figure 4-2a. Keep your elbows straight. This is hard. You will be surprised at the strength required. Try for five. When you can do ten, add two more boards. If you don't have them, work up to fifteen.

Walking the Wall. Facing the side of the pool, grab the edge of pool with your hands. Place your feet flat on the side of the pool and walk up the wall until you can go no further. Walk down. Start with five. (See Figure 4-2b.)

Back-stretching. This can be done standing or floating. Standing, bring your bent knee to your waist. Grab it with your arm and pull tight. Bend your head to the knee. Repeat with opposite leg. Be sure to keep exercising leg within shoulder line. Super for the back. Do ten.

Leg Circles. Have your back against the pool wall. Extend your arms and hold on to the wall. Pick up your feet and extend them in front of you. Keeping your back as flat as possible, rotate your legs in circles. Good for waist and tough on arms. Start with five.

Flutter-kicking with Kickboard. Hold board two-thirds of the way up. Keep your elbows straight, shoulders slightly under water, and eyes looking straight ahead. Push off bottom and flutter kick with legs *very slightly* bent, remembering to think, kick *up*. Feel the water pressing on the backs of your legs and on the soles of your feet. The front of kickboard should be kept at a slight upward angle. Do not put your weight on the board. If you get "stuck" and don't go anywhere, put your feet down and start over. Don't be discouraged; I've had women take weeks to accomplish 50 yards. Start with ten yards and repeat five times. Increase as much as you want.

Kickboard Rowing. Sit on kickboard. This is a neat trick. Practice a few times. Sideways works best, with your seat hanging over about an inch or two and your legs from knee down just hanging. Use your arms as if rowing. Front and back. Do ten yards each way and repeat five times. (See Figure 4-2c.) How was that? My ladies loves these!

145

What to Do About Hair, Skin, Eyes, Ears, and Nose

There are always questions about little things that can make the difference between happy swimmers and unhappy swimmers. Here are some typical ones.

Hair

Question: My hair is long and bothers me when I swim. What can I do about it?
Answer: If it is very long, braid it. Braids keep the hair out of your face and out of the pool. Shoulder length hair does well in pony tails, but use the coated rubber bands. Bathing caps are sometimes satisfactory, the best one being the light-weight stretchy one the racers wear. Don't expect it to keep your hair dry, though.

Question: What do you suggest for blonde hair that turns green after swimming?
Answer: A daily shampoo with a mild shampoo and a once-a-week rinse with 3% hydrogen peroxide.

Question: Is it true that swimming and sun are bad for your hair?
Answer: They haven't been bad for mine! I color my hair now and it does fade quickly; but I still have a lot of nice thick, healthy hair; and I average five hours a day in the water for a period of six to eight months a year.

Skin

Question: What is the correct way to buy a sunscreen?
Answer: Analyze your sensitivity to the sun and shop for the desired protection. As of 1979 sunscreen products are rated to designate their protection factor (SPF). A SPF of 3 means if you use the product you can stay in the sun three times longer with it than without it, without burning. The highest rating is SPF 19. If you are fair and want to block out most of the sun, shop for a creamy or thick-consistency product, rated at SPF 19.

Question: What stays on best in the water?
Answer: A thick, or creamy-type, preparation resists water

146

better than the alcohol-based products. However, the latter are fine for those not getting wet. Apply to all exposed areas, especially bald spots, noses, ears, lips, and *backs of hands.*

Question: Must I always wear a sunscreen?

Answer: Before 10:00 A.M. and after 4:00 P.M. the sun's rays are less harmful, and unless you are very sensitive early morning and late afternoon are fairly safe times to get a little tan.

Question: What do you do for extra-sensitive areas?

Answer: I am a fair, freckled redhead and have to be extra careful. After 10:00 A.M. I use moisturizer, a sun block cream with a SPF of 19, and then a coat of my favorite cream-type foundation on my face and on the backs of my hands. On my lips I use a sun block cream or stick and then a dark cream lipstick with sunscreen. My arms and back tan reasonably well and a 9 SPF cream seems to be adequate. It has to be reapplied about every three hours. If I don't wipe my face, the protective products I use will last six to eight hours.

Question: What about babies in the sun?

Answer: Use a sun block product with a SPF of 19, and keep a bonnet or cap on their heads if they are in the sun more than twenty minutes during the period from 10:00 A.M. to 4:00 P.M. I have seen serious complications from infant sunburn so restrict sunning to early and late in the day and use caution at all times.

Eyes

Question: Why do my eyes burn under water?

Answer: Poor water chemistry (chlorine too high or the pH too low), irritation existing in the eye, or excessive rubbing can cause your eyes to burn.

Question: What can I do about it?

Answer: Complain to your pool manager; check for any signs of existing infection; wipe off your eyebrows and forehead when coming up instead of rubbing your eyelids.

Question: Do drops help?

Answer: Some racers will use a drop of mineral oil before swimming and an over-the-counter product afterward. However, it doesn't seem to help a great deal.

Question: What about goggles?

Answer: If all else fails, use them but remember not to jump or dive with them on. Almost all competitors wear them now because of the speed at which they move and length of time they are in the water. It's better to use goggles than to swim with your eyes closed or with your head up!

Ears

Question: What is swimmer's ear?

Answer: It is a fungal infection of the outer ear caused by water not draining out of the ear. The fungus produces a substance that causes itching, inflammation, and pain.

Question: Can it be prevented?

Answer: Yes. Ask your druggist to mix you a solution of drops to use or buy a ready-mixed one that will lower the pH and prevent fungal growth. If you have the symptoms already, these drops won't help; you'll need medication from your doctor.

Question: Does everyone get it?

Answer: No. With all the hours I spend in the water, I've only had it twice in the last twenty years.

Question: So many children have tubes in their ears. I've heard they cannot get their ears wet. Does this mean they cannot swim?

Answer: It is an individual thing. For certain children some doctors will prescribe ear plugs made from a mold of each ear. Many of my babies swim with them and have no problems.

Question: Should I buy ear plugs at the store if we are going to swim a lot?

Answer: By all means no. The ordinary ear is a marvelous, intricate piece of equipment and handles water well without assistance. Plugs can be dangerous and can also help cause infection. Check with your physician.

Question: Sometimes after swimming my ears feel plugged up. What causes this?

Answer: Water in the canal. Drop a few drops of rubbing alcohol into each ear. As it drains out, it will bring some water with it and will evaporate the rest. Do not try to get the water out by sticking your fingers or anything else into the ear.

Question: I have sinus trouble, but love to swim. What should I do?

Answer: Wear a nose clip; get one of the little ones used by the synchronized swimmers available at sporting goods stores. Refrain from diving.

Question: Can people with asthma and allergies participate in water sports?

Answer: Yes. Swimming can be especially beneficial to those so afflicted. Check with your doctor for individual restrictions.

Overall Guidelines for Healthy Swimming

Question: Generally speaking, when can you swim or not swim?

Answer: Do not swim when you have a fever, a rash from an unknown cause, boils, or infected wounds. Do not swim with "pink eye," intestinal disturbances, or a fresh cold (first 36 hours).

Competitive Swimming

America's swimmers have become leaders in international competition because of an excellent age-group swimming program. It was developed in the early 1950s to train young swimmers who might have the potential to develop into national champions or world-class athletes. More than 500,000 youngsters between the ages of six and seventeen train and compete each year in the various programs and events that are set up and controlled by the Amateur Athletic Union of the United States. Although only about 1% become world-class competitors, the rest derive great benefit from the sport and do a lot to promote swimming on a local and neighborhood level all over the United States.

The children compete only within their age groups which are: eight and under, nine to ten year olds, eleven to twelve year olds, thirteen to fourteen year olds, and fifteen to seventeen year olds.

When a competitor can meet the qualifying time requirements and has had a twelfth birthday, he is eligible for **149** the senior competition which is open to anyone over the age of twelve.

Most outstanding swimmers are under twenty-five years of age. Until recently if you had reached that ripe old age you had no one to train with or race against. Now an age-group program has been put together for the "old folks," which keeps them in the swim until they are eighty and over. It is called the Master's Program and is growing rapidly. It keeps former athletes from dropping out of their sport and gives a new interest to many new enthusiasts. When you reach the point where you can swim 500 yards you are more than ready. For information call your local YMCA or swim club.

The Pros and Cons of Age-Group Swimming

As a coach for more than twenty years and as a mother of four state champions, I still favor the age-group program because it is an individual effort with team support. Bringing up a child in the swimming program is very beneficial to him. I cannot think of a better way to train a child for life mentally and, at the same time, to develop physical skills important to his future, health, and safety. By working out regularly, the swimmer builds muscles to protect his body should he elect to play contact sports later on. He develops coordination in all areas. He builds confidence and learns to cope with stress. The relationship of success to hard work is obvious, and his knowledge of that soon carries over into everything he does.

Unlike in some sports, no swimmers sit on the bench. At a swimming meet every child is allowed to compete in the events offered.

Team swimming enables the child to build the strength (mental, physical, and emotional), confidence, and endurance necessary to reach a goal. In addition, anyone who swims with a team for a year or two will be much safer than those who don't.

The entire family becomes involved when a member joins a team. It takes almost 100 volunteer parents and **150** workers to put on a meet. During the season, almost every weekend is spent with father timing and mother place judging or working in the records office. Soon the other children are eager to be part of the action. Training diets, disqualifications, coaches, and times become prime topics for discussion.

So far so good. All of this enriches the family life. If Mom and Dad can just resist the temptation to be parents of a "real winner" everything will be fine.

The most harmful things in the age-group program are the overeager parent and the overly ambitious coach. These two promote, push, nag, and sometimes belittle or verbally whip their athletes in order to make them winners. It takes inspiration, not humiliation to produce a champion.

In my opinion harm is also done by allowing children to compete at too young an age. I have coached many children six years old and under but only because the parents expected it. I believe that a child should be seven years old before joining a team, and he should not compete until he can perform comfortably and without embarrassment.

When your child has learned to swim twenty-five to fifty yards of the crawl and the backstroke with ease and expresses an interest in competition, call the local swim clubs. Inquire about their teams. Plan to attend a workout and talk with the coach. Look for a happy, well-disciplined team where the swimmers appear eager to be in the water. The coach should be on deck and visibly participating in running the show with humor and good will. An age-group coach has a difficult job. He can never forget that the program exists for the benefit of the child. Personal ambitions have to come in second place for coaches and parents, and they must work together to develop the swimmer without undue pressure.

When you have selected the team and coach that appear most suitable to you and your child, turn your child over to the coach and relax. If you have questions about your child's progress or any part of the program, call and make an appointment. Coaches cannot talk at all well during a workout.

The first month of training is difficult and your child may become disheartened. Encourage him and try to make sure that he does not miss any workouts. Once he is in better condition and has become used to the disciplined effort, he will love it. Nearly all youngsters really enjoy all aspects of

151

swimming on a team. That is why we have nearly 500,000 children in the program.

Remember that the real goal is steady improvement and not victory, sweet though it may be. Pierre Coubertin, founder of the modern Olympics, put it well when he said, "It is not the victory, but the struggle that counts." So hang loose, Mom and Dad. Let the coach and your offspring move at their own speed. You will be excited and pleased with the results.

How to Be a Good Team Parent

- See that your child gets to the required workouts on time. It is necessary for the swimmers to get to the pool in time for the warm-up.
- Plan nutritious meals.
- Provide opportunity for adequate rest.
- Maintain communication with the coach.
- Do not analyze and criticize your child's swimming. Let the coach do the coaching.
- Do not dispute the decision of the judges. If something puzzles or disturbs you, tell your coach at once.
- Support your coach. If you disagree with him, do not discuss it in front of your child. They have to work together every day and need to feel good about each other. Go directly to the coach with your concerns.
- Find a local physician who is experienced in sports medicine so you know whom to consult should there be any physical problems. Many illnesses and injuries are surmounted by today's athletes.
- Do your part in working at the meets, providing transportation, and raising money, cheerfully.
- Learn what reasonable improvements to look for in your child. Make a goal chart and reward the goals attained. This is best if done on a monthly basis.
- Above all do not belittle any effort. Do not withhold love if your child falls short of your expectations.

5

Extracurricular Fun

The lure of other activities will call to you once you are a swimmer. Boating is one that attracts lots of families and it is no wonder. There are boats for every place, everyone, and every thing—paddle, sail, inboard, or outboard: small, medium, or large, safe enough for a family or daring enough for the adventurer. The selection of a boat is even more complicated than selecting the right pool for your yard. It won't boggle your mind quite so much if you go about your selection in the now-familiar method of orderly progressions.

Have Your Own Boats, Skis, Snorkels

How to Select the Right Boat

- Talk to your friends who have boats.
- Visit marinas and yacht clubs.
- Attend boat shows.
- Ask your friends who have boats to let you go out on a short trip with them.
- Go to a fishing camp and rent various boats—even a canoe and a row boat.
- Inquire about local boat registration laws and insurance costs.
- Be sure you have a place to keep a boat.
- Check all safety features. Look especially for adequate freeboard and a deep transom.

When you have decided about the type you want, look at the used boats advertised in the newspapers and boating magazines. There is a saying among yachtsmen that the two happiest people in the world are the man who just sold a boat and the man who just bought one! You can save a great deal of money and still get a fine, safe boat by buying a used one. Boats that have been well cared for are good for years and years. There is even a certain amount of pride that is bought along with an older sailboat that has weathered well.

Be sure to investigate the kits available for the do-it-yourself craftsman. Many different hulls are available that can be finished to satisfy your personal needs. Your boat dealers can give you information or send you to a company that supplies the parts.

Our family has a Sunfish, an aluminum outboard skiff, **155** and a twenty-two-foot sloop. We used to have a ski-boat and a little twelve-foot sailing "pram." It is hard to describe the feeling one gets for the family boats. We have loved them all! Right now the quiet beauty of the sail-powered vessels appeals to us. The equally quiet and amazingly versatile canoe is also fascinating. To each his own! For thrills, adventure, and never-ending variety, boating is tops.

Figure 5-1. *John comes aboard like a pirate.*

Boating Adventures for Hire

It is possible to arrange white-water canoe trips (or floats), American or European yacht charters, and Windjammer Cruises all over the world. Travel agents can assist you in locating such trips, as can boat manufacturers and travel magazines.

Tips for Boating Safety

- Remember, the skipper is in command.
- Keep your boat in good condition.
- Have all required safety equipment on board. Arrange for a Coast Guard inspection. (It's free.)
- Do not overload your boat or go out in an overloaded boat. Check the capacity plate for details.

156

- Take advantage of the United States Power Squadron or Coast Guard Auxiliary boating safety classes.
- Know your local weather patterns. Pay attention to weather bulletins, and don't fight the weather. Learn to patiently wait for storms to blow over.
- Study charts of the area where you will be boating.
- Be familiar with your life jackets and practice wearing them in the water.

Figure 5-2a-b. *Power squadron rendezvous.*

(a)

(b)

Figure 5-3. *Sail ho!*

- If you fall overboard or if your boat capsizes, stay in the area or with the boat.
- Do not allow bow riding. Your children and even your friends may beg to do this but it is so dangerous that for your own protection you *must* prohibit it.

Masks, Snorkel, and Fins

Watching the underwater world is a thrilling pastime, and it can be done with a mask, snorkel, and fins. Consult an experienced diver or a certified underwater instructor if you need help on obtaining the best possible fit.

158   The human eye does not see very well underwater, but a face mask changes this by locking in an airspace between the eye and the water. The mask should be made of shatterproof glass set in a soft neoprene or rubber skirt. Hard rubber skirts should be avoided because they do not conform as well to the contours of the face. Tinted and plastic faceplates should also be avoided. Goggles, which are popular with the competitive and fitness swimmers, distort the vision and are not as satisfactory as the single plate of glass.

Before buying a mask, place it on your face without the strap. Inhale slightly through your nose. The mask should remain in place. With the strap on it should be comfortable and not leave red marks or irritate the skin. Do not compromise on the fit or quality of a face mask. Leaks are a nuisance as well as a danger.

The snorkel, a J-shaped tube of rubber or plastic 16 to 18 inches long, is what the snorkeldiver breathes through. It has a soft rubber mouthpiece (bit) on one end, and the other end extends up out of the water. It is held to your mask with a little rubber ring.

It is easy to learn how to inhale slowly and exhale sharply to clear the tube of water. Snorkeling is simple because you don't have to turn or lift your head to breathe.

Fins are the other piece of equipment you will need, and they too should be properly fitted. There are two kinds: open-heel fins and full-foot fins. I prefer the full-foot fin, but if you like the other type buy boots to wear under them to prevent chafing. All divers, even snorkel divers, should have some form of flotation equipment and a diving flag if snorkeling is going to be done in the open water. There are many varieties available, and your scuba dealer or instructor will be able to advise you on what is best for you. Be sure to get them because in most states diving without a flag is illegal, and it does spoil the fun if you get a citation and have to pay a fine! Figure 5-4 shows how to kick when using fins.

With your mask, snorkel, and fins you can swim along on the surface and be a Peeping Tom looking at the fascinating creatures and plants below you. You can also use them for your fitness swims if you cannot master the normal breathing skills. Of course, if you use fins and snorkels you would have to increase your distance somewhat. Keep in mind that twenty minutes of sustained effort is what it takes to condition the cardiovascular system.

Figure 5-4. *How to kick with fins.*

Your children will enjoy this sport too, but be extremely particular about buying their equipment. It is worth the time and money to buy safety glass, properly fitting masks, and the full-foot fins.

Figure 5-5. *Photographer Steve does a self-portrait.*

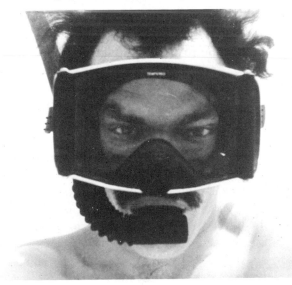

Scuba is an abbreviation for Self-Contained Underwater Breathing Apparatus. Man has been fascinated by the underwater world since 3,000 B.C. Today, thanks to fine equipment it is possible to spend hours beneath the surface enjoying the sights and sounds of this other world.

One does not rush into this sport and must learn to swim *well* before signing up for the necessary instructions. Most states require certification of all persons seeking to fill their scuba tanks with air, so before you can participate in this adventure you have to find an instructor certified by the National Association of Underwater Instructors, take the course, and pass it. Your local YMCA or sporting goods dealer can tell you how to locate an instructor.

When you are certified and experienced, there are special tours and trips available that will offer you an opportunity to explore the seas of the world. Perhaps you will find a sunken pirate ship or the remains of an ancient civilization. Check with your travel agent!

Waterskiing

Waterskiing is a sport for speed-lovers. It's thrilling, not too difficult, and most of my friends who ski were taught by their friends. Many people who are ski-enthusiasts make a hobby of teaching others, so if you are interested in learning find a buddy who is willing to help you.

Be sure, however, to observe some precautions. Too many people ski without knowing how to swim! Please master the Rest and treading water before going out on this adventure.

- Wear your ski belt or vest at all times.
- Avoid heavily traveled areas.
- Be confident in the skipper of the boat pulling you.
- Have a third person in the boat to watch you and handle the rope.
- Learn the hand signals.
- Avoid skiing too long at a time.

161

Living by the Water

For many of us living by the water is a dream come true. The changing panorama of nature's moods makes life exciting. However, there are precautions that must be taken, especially if you have young children.

- Adequate fencing, with locks, must be installed.
- All adults and older family members should know how to swim, do the survival skills, make elementary rescues, and give mouth-to-mouth resuscitation.
- Ring buoys, ropes, and pole should be kept on the pier or by the waterfront at all times.
- All young children should learn to swim and should be taught to respect the water.
- A few sensible family rules should be agreed on and enforced.
- Piers must be kept in good repair.
- Children playing or fishing on the pier should wear their arm floats or life jackets. Inflatable water wings are NOT a lifesaving device, but they are better than a discarded bulky life jacket. Young children should not play on the pier alone.
- Have practice sessions to be sure everyone knows what to do in an emergency.

Swim in Your Own Backyard

With the complications of energy shortages, expensive vacations, and life in general, the family swimming pool is becoming more and more feasible. Many people ask if I think they should have a pool. Ninety-nine percent of the time my answer is yes!

If you are young and have no children, a pool is great for exercising and partying. If you are young and have a family, a pool keeps them busy, hungry, and tired. It may keep you busy, hungry, and tired, too; but that's better than being bored, fat, and lazy!

As the family grows older they become capable of taking over the chores and some of the partying, but the family group can still stay fit and enjoy swimming together. A pool is a great gathering place and encourages the family to hang around home instead of someplace else.

When you are old and the children have left you can *still* work out, float around, and go skinny dipping.

Even the arthritic, crippled, and paralyzed can benefit from exercising in a pool.

Everyone regardless of age or condition can enjoy a pool at home where it is accessible at dawn, dusk, and moonrise.

Types of Pools

There is a pool for every pocketbook as well as pools in a variety of designs and materials. However, pools are generally classified as above-ground or in-ground pools. Leave it to my family to be different! Ours is half above the ground and half in the ground. You can select anything from vinyl, fiberglass, stainless steel, or concrete. Your choice will depend on your budget and on the property on which it is to be built. Every locale has qualities that require careful evaluation before you make your final selection.

Prices vary in about the same price range as automobiles, and you should shop for a pool in the same way as you shop for a car. Be positive that you shop only at reputable dealers. Follow all the normal cautious procedures. Inspect pools he has built and talk to the owners. Sign a contract when you are satisfied with the builder's integrity, and get ready to enjoy life in a new terrific way!

Fall and winter are the best times to shop for a pool. Some builders will give a considerable discount on pools built during the off-season.

If you are a do-it-yourselfer, there are kits available for pools that you and your family can build without a great deal of difficulty. It is usually wise to hire a good backhoe operator, electrician, and plumber. It is possible to save up to 50% of the total cost. Check with your local building officials to find out what requirements are necessary to satisfy them. A building permit and inspections are usually standard procedure.

163

- Access to pool site
- Availability of utility hookups
- Location of trees, septic tanks, underground cables, and so on.
- Access to pool from house
- Direction of prevailing winds
- Location of overhead wires
- Types of soil and potential for underground water or rocks
- Local building ordinances
- Location, size, shape, and depth preferences
- Price range
- Local and state insurance requirements
- Fire department to see if they will fill pool when its finished.

It's a good idea to check all the above and then lay your garden hose out on the ground where you think you want to put the pool. Look at it for a few days and change it around until it pleases you. A free-form shape may suit your yard better than a traditional rectangle so don't be afraid to be creative. Just be sure to meet all code requirements.

We are extremely happy with our present pool and find it fills our needs adequately. It is a 16′ × 32-foot vinyl lined pool with a constant sidewall depth of four feet. It is deep enough for us to swim our laps, but shallow enough for all but the younger swimmers to stand up in. There are four eight-foot-wide steps on one end to give the littlest ones a place to swim and play.

We had to choose between a greatly increased cost and a shallow pool because we discovered water almost as soon as we began digging the hole. Since the pool is about twenty-five yards from Biloxi Bay, we were not surprised.

I have access to deep water pools for teaching, so our pool suits the site and our needs well. If you plan on having deep water and a diving board, have your dealer check the current recommendations of the National Swimming Pool Institute and abide by them.

My husband John, our daughter Merileigh, and I built **164** our pool in a week in 1976. To commemorate the great bicentennial year, we wrote an inscription in the concrete part of the deck. Everyone who comes, chuckles at our foolishness, that is, everyone except Christiana. She tested her first-grade reading ability for a few seconds then wrinkled up her face and inquired anxiously. "Bubs, is somebody *buried* there?"

Is Having a Pool Worth the Trouble?

Yes! And if you don't agree after your first sunrise or moonlight swim, I'll be surprised. There is absolutely nothing to compare with the peace, quiet, and beauty of a dip when everyone else is tucked away!

The problems of maintenance are real, but with all the new equipment, materials, and products, they are no longer awesome. As a matter of fact you can have a pool that is virtually automatic. There are several things that should be checked daily for trouble-free operation, but automatic shut-off systems prevent anything drastic from happening if you are out of town or preoccupied.

Daily Checklist for Pool Operators (Papa-Mama-Family?)

1. Check skimmer baskets (the basket that collects the leaves and particles of dust and so on that blow into the pool). Empty if necessary. *Note:* Is suction good?
2. Check water where it comes into pool. Is flow good?
3. Read filter pressure gauge. Is it operating at normal pressure?
4. Use test kit to check water chemistry. Are the sanitizer readings correct?
5. Does pool need vacuuming?

Your pool builder will instruct you specifically on how to keep your pool sparkling and beautiful. Once you understand how everything works, you will be able to take care of the pool easily. Most residential pools need backwashing and vacuuming once a week unless there is a storm or you have a lot of visitors.

Water chemistry needs to be checked daily. Depending on your budget, you can do this yourselves, buy automatic

165

equipment, or hire a pool service company. Caring for your pool is not difficult, but it must be done on a regular basis.

Control

The other problem that concerns people thinking about buying their own pool is how to avoid being overrun by the neighborhood children. There are some good solutions.

1. Allow no children under _____ years (set your age limit) to swim without a parent.
2. Fix a place where you can fly a flag. When the flag flies, properly chaperoned company is welcome. When the flag is down, the pool is for private use only.
3. Decide on a *few* sensible rules to swim by and enforce them.

Remember: one of the reasons for having a pool is to make home more attractive to your children and their friends. So do a little lifeguarding, it's better than wondering where everyone is!

Our only regret about our pool is that we took twenty years to build one at home!

6

Safety:
First, Last,
and Always

The secrets of safety are to be in control of your environment and to know your family's capabilities. Set a good example yourself; set sensible limits and be prepared for any emergency.

Safety is a habit and the best way to become safe is to learn the safety skills and rules yourself. By setting good safe examples, we can make safety a habit for our children. I firmly believe that even the old folks should try to conquer fears, to adjust to the water, and to become capable of enjoying aquatic activities. Sure, it may be a nuisance to be consistent but habits are built by consistency, so you may have to suffer for awhile. This is the way I think it should happen:

1. Father and mother should learn to swim.
2. Babies and young children should have swimming lessons yearly from six months until they are seven years old, then swim on a team at least until they are old enough to take a lifesaving course (eleven years old).
3. Children under five years old should never be in the water *without a parent or responsible, mature person* IN the water with them.
4. Children five to eleven years old should have a responsible person on the deck.
5. Children over eleven years old should take the Red Cross or YMCA lifesaving instruction and should swim only in places with a guard in authority.
6. If the family is going boating or camping and anticipates swimming where there are no guards, it is imperative to take your own lifeguard (one of your own group should be capable). Rescues should be rehearsed before the trip and should be practiced with a certified instructor to check you out. It may be impractical to require all fathers to have a Red Cross certificate, but it is not unrealistic to have someone teach mother and father and big brothers and sisters how to rescue family members.
7. Check with local authorities about swimming areas before making trip.
8. Stay in good physical condition.
9. Take proper safety equipment with you. This should   **169**

include: *Life jackets that fit* (one each!), rope, ring buoy, and a first aid kit.

Setting the Limits

Advance planning of your time will make your outing much more pleasant and safer, too. Before getting to the pool, beach, campground, or out on your boat agree where, when, with whom, and how long everyone will swim. Designate the family lifeguard, if you are away from normally guarded areas. Most hotel and motel pools do not use regular lifeguards, so if you are swimming in a hotel pool, be sure you have one person assigned to be on watch. It is not difficult for excitement and confusion to result in parents going to the room and leaving a child behind. The buddy system is helpful. It means that each person has a "buddy" who is never out of reach. When the guard calls, "buddy check," the two buddies grab hands and raise them until the guard acknowledges them. Camps and municipal pools have used the system successfully for years.

Decide who can swim in deep areas and who must stay in the shallow water. Plan a resting period out of the water about every forty-five minutes. Dry off, relax, and read, or play quiet games for fifteen or twenty minutes. A light snack (fruit or cookie) might be in order too. Parents tell me they can't get the children out of the water, and I have seen three-year-olds throw tantrums over it, but remember that children do not have much judgment. It is *very* important not to get overtired or too sunburned. If these rules are established in advance, there is seldom a problem.

Eliminate Surprises

Learn the following skills *together* and practice them until you can execute them comfortably.

1. Jump and dive into deep water and return to side.
2. Walk from shallow water to deep water, turn, and swim back.

3. The Rest until you can maintain yourselves up to thirty minutes. The teenagers and adults should try for an hour. Offer a good reward for this.

4. The use of your life jackets.

5. Elementary Rescues:
   a. Throw a rope
   b. Throw rope and buoy
   c. Use of a pole
   d. Arm and leg extension
   e. Tired swimmer carry
   f. The best way for you to support your young child and swim.
   g. Treading water up to fifteen minutes.

6. Check all toys, inflatables, and scuba gear to make sure everything is in repair.

7. When not swimming at a pool, check all the tidal conditions before getting in.

8. Try out life jackets to make certain that they fit and that everyone knows how to wear one.

NOTE: Buying a PFD (Personal Flotation Device) for children under five is difficult. Most life jackets are designed to keep the wearer on his back. This is fine if a child is unconscious but can be very frightening if he has never been on his back before. Practice back floating and finning with the whole family. Wear your jackets once a month or so to become familiar. Do *NOT* use them to swim in, under ordinary circumstances. If the jacket comes up over child's ears, tips him over, or restricts arm movement too much, try another. Some jackets use weight as a guide to proper sizing, others use chest measurement. After testing several kinds, I have concluded that very few are totally satisfactory for *little* children. Even jackets that are labeled "this jacket is designed to hold a conscious person in a vertical position" do not do so. Since young children are so distressed by being on their backs, which is what jackets are supposed to do, it is difficult to find a satisfactory life jacket. Please try different types before you buy one. After you purchase one, practice with it enough so that your little ones learn what to expect. *Do not swim in it on a regular basis!*

The United States Coast Guard has weight specification recommendations for childrens' use of the type II and **171** type III PFDs. You should try a friend's jackets on your children and also use the Coast Guard recommendations in determining the proper PFDs for your children. (See Figure 6-1a–c.) After watching quite a few very small children in the type II PFD, I can only urge you to start your child's water education early. Help him become used to being on his back in the water by encouraging bathtub activity from the time he is *tiny* and by letting him get his face and eyes wet without wiping them dry instantly. The type I PFD is for adults for use in open water. Sea-going liners and commercial fishing boats are required to provide them.

The restraining and backward affects created by the PFDs are necessary, but they are disturbing to a youngster who has had no indoctrination to the water.

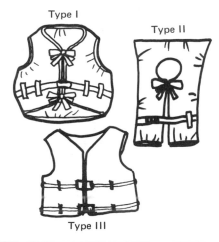

Figure 6-1a-c. *Personal flotation devices. (a) Type I. (b) Type II. (c) Type III.*

Build These Habits

1. Enter the water *with* your preschooler or be sure a totally responsible person goes in with him. Enter hand in hand or with him in arms, as suitable.

2. Enter where it is shallow and get adjusted to and familiar with the situation. Don't assume everything will always be the same depth, temperature, and so on. A difference of two or three inches can be tremendous to a two-year-old.

3. Refrain from constantly getting in and out; your child can run and jump in at the other end before you can get there.

4. Respond immediately to commands from lifeguards or parents and to requests from children or inexperienced swimmers. (If they say no, honor it; if they ask for help, give it.)

5. Always know where your group is. Be sure to tell someone if you are getting out or going to another area.

6. Be alert to each other's needs.

7. Do not chew gum (or tobacco) or eat while in the water; it's too easy to choke.

The purpose of rule number 1 is to teach children that the onl way to go into the water is with an older person. The purpose of rule number 2 is to teach that running and jumping into the water at any old place is not safe. All water should be entered after an evaluation of the circumstances.

Control the Environment

If you are going to the beach, pick the time of day when the tide, currents, and sun are best suited to your family. Listen to weather reports and pay attention to small craft advisories, thunderstorms, and the like.

Pools also vary in conditions. Choose a time when the crowd, the weather, and the water appeal to you the most.

If you have a pool at home, you can have total control of fencing, temperature, chemicals, and people. The weather is the only thing you can't handle.

A funny story comes to mind everytime I think about weather. A Catholic priest used to come to my big indoor pool to work out every day. One day when the wintery weather had kept everyone away, he commented on the lack of swimmers. "This isn't too good for business, is it?" he said. I agreed and suggested he put in a good word for me and see if he could stop the rain. His ready reply was, "Sorry, I'm in sales, not management!"

173

When you can't control the environment enough to have a pleasant and safe swim, wait until another time.

More Questions and Answers

Question: Is mother or father the best person to teach a child to swim?

Answer: It doesn't matter which parent does the job. The baby six months to a year old usually feels more secure with its mother, but if the father is available and willing, there is no reason why he cannot be a fine teacher.

Question: Do fathers and mothers go about teaching in the same way?

Answer: No. Most men come on much too fast and much too strong. They do not seem to be able to put themselves in the place of the student. Engineers, scientists, and doctors seem more willing to analyze, explain, and understand than are athletes, lawyers, and teachers. Sometimes it is harder for the men to follow instructions than it is for the women.

On the other hand, many women are much too protective; and without realizing that they are doing it, they create and reinforce uneasiness and fear in their children by cuddling them excessively, by holding them in different than normal positions, and by repeating reassuring words used in situations the child knows are not good. A matter-of-fact, logical, patient approach is best, and the parent whose personality is more suited should do the teaching.

Question: My two-year-old clings to me and hangs on to my neck tightly as soon as we get in the water. What should I do?

Answer: Let him cling to you, but do not cling to him. Hold him just as if you were walking down the street (securely but not clutching). Get low in the water and walk, talking about lunch or some familiar topic of interest. When he sees that you are not clinging or comforting him, he will begin to ease his grip. Soon you will be able to work him around to the kicking position and start the instruction.

Question: I like to swim in water where my feet touch the bottom, but get panicky the minute I know I am in water over

174 my head. What should I do to get over this?

Answer: Learn the Rest and to tread water; practice one stroke until you have mastered the breathing well enough to swim twenty yards in deep water without stopping. Keep increasing the distance little by little. Have a capable friend swim beside you. Repeat. Repeat. *Remember:* You can *walk* in shallow water, but you *have to swim in the deep!*

Question: What should a swimmer do if he gets a cramp?

Answer: Stretch the cramped area as much as possible, to allow blood to circulate better. Breathe deeply and regularly, massage gently—*away from the heart,* and keep swimming. Return to shallow water. Cramps are usually caused by improper warm-up and lack of oxygen in the muscle. If they occur frequently, they could be caused by dietery deficiencies; you should check with your doctor to see if you are getting enough calcium, potassium, and other elements. A cramp definitely does not have to spell disaster, but it does need attention.

Question: What does it mean when I get a pain in my side ("a stitch") after swimming a few laps?

Answer: All athletes are bothered by this at one time or another. No one knows the exact cause, but most probably it comes from starting out too fast. Do more stretching exercises before starting and increase your warm-up period. Increase your speed gradually.

Question: My child cries when we get into the water. What should I do?

Answer: I wish I knew why some children cry. Generally, two-year-olds cry in protest; babies cry in uneasiness or discomfort; older children cry because they have learned that they can get their way by crying, or, once in a while, they cry from honest fear. Use distraction, and a positive approach. Don't overreact. If crying persists, get out for a few minutes and try again. Taking turns doing a simple skill helps.

In an effort to stop a youngster's howling (no tears), I gazed in his opened mouth and proclaimed, with authority, "I see *your* teeth." More howling was the reply. I tried again. "Now I can see your tonsils!" A look of indignation crossed his face, and he stated firmly, "Oh, *no,* you don't. *It's* underwater!" He did not open his mouth again to cry and swims beautifully now, just because he thought it was bad for me to see his tonsils! *Remember:* Just keep trying and don't wage war!

175

Question: What should I do if my child says that he doesn't want to learn to swim?

Answer: You shouldn't ask him! Children should assume that they will have swimming lessons, just as they assume they will go to school. There should be no choice. Lessons should start by age four and continue until the teen years. Schools and communities should include swimming programs; if they don't, teach as much as you feel comfortable teaching, using this book as a guide, then find good instructors or a swim team and pay the price. It is worth it.

Question: What is the most difficult skill to teach a child?

Answer: Breathing is the most difficult skill to *learn* or to *teach.* Babies and adults alike become tired and frustrated while mastering the art of taking a breath while swimming. And so, may I add, do the instructors!

The first thing you must teach a little one about taking a breath is how to hold his breath. Humming, holding his nose gently, and repeating "no, no sniff, sniff" all help make the explanation. After the child has been swimming in your wake a few times, tell him that he is going to swim while you count to five and then you will pick him up so he can take a breath and then you'll let him swim again. Establish the rhythm (one, two, three, four, five, take a breath; one, two, three, four, five, take a breath) and keep it constant. It is reassuring for the child to know that you will always pick him up at the same time to breathe.

Give him time. Watch him carefully. Do not let go of him until he takes a breath. Keep moving. Do not lift him any higher out of the water than necessary for him to take a breath. Use one hand on his upper arm to lift him. Then progress to one hand under his tummy. Then tell him that when he is ready to breathe, to hold your hand and lift himself up. Keep your hand available and ready to support him. Count. If he does not come up by himself on the "five," lift him barely high enough to grab a breath and let him go. (See Figure 6-2a–e.)

Sometimes you may have to explain that there is no time to wipe his eyes or hair off his face. You will have to teach him to bubble, bubble, bubble, bubble, bubble, after he has gotten familiar and comfortable with all the other aspects of breathing, and then it will all begin to fall together.

Coordinating your movements with those of the child is

Figure 6-2a-e. *More about breathing. (a) Lift child with one hand on his chest. (b) Lift by chin (difficult with some). (c) Ben is using my hand to lift himself. (d) After the five-count, tap child on head to signal him to lift his head and breathe. (e) Keep your hand up for him to focus on. Put it back underwater and repeat.*

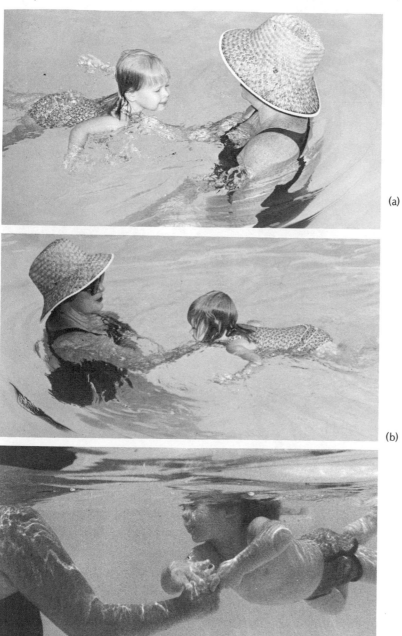

(a)

(b)

(c)

(d)

(e)

difficult, and it is fortunate that children are quite durable because the first few times mama or papa usually messes up. If you do, don't give any indication that it bothers you. Don't repeat the routine more than twice (going about thirty feet) each time for the first four or five lessons that you do it. By then both you and your little one should be familiar with the routine and capable of repeating it several times. Stop when your child shows any signs of fatigue or unhappiness.

The biggest problem here is caused by not giving the child a long enough time to breathe. It takes awhile to send all the signals to the brain so don't *rush* him.

178   *Question:* Who were the first swimmers?

Answer: Millions of years ago our ancestors lived in beautiful forests. The rain was frequent and lush fruit-bearing plants provided them with plenty to eat, with places to hide, and with shade to play in. Then little by little it stopped raining. Trees died. Food became scarce and hungry enemies attacked. In an effort to escape, these ancient creatures ran and ran. After awhile they came to the sea. There was no other place to go to hide so they ran into the water. It felt strange, but wonderfully cool, and their enemies did not follow. So our relatives of long ago began to spend their days in the water and their nights in caves. They learned to swim and to catch and eat fish and shellfish. The babies held on to their mother's long hair and paddled around happily sometimes under, sometimes on top of the water. Maybe these babies were the very first swimmers.

Elaine Morgan hypothesizes in her book, *Descent of Woman* (Stein and Day, 1972), that the ancestors of man sought the water as relief from the drought and heat of the Pliocene Age by living in the water by day and caves by night. The mamas, missing the big teeth of the papas, were quite defenseless, they had to flee into the water to survive. They adapted to this in many interesting ways, according to Ms. Morgan, and after twelve million years left the sea and made their way on earth. Those that remained in the water continued adapting and are known today as porpoises and manatees. Fascinating, isn't it?

The cavemen continued to swim, and they fished for pleasure as well as for the necessity of catching food. I believe that they enjoyed their aquatic activities as families today do, and I picture the children and their mothers playing in the water while the men fished and hunted nearby.

As time went on, life became more sophisticated, and people began to draw pictures and keep records of their daily activities. For instance, we know that about four thousand years ago there was a man who lived in Egypt who was secretary to the pharaoh and wrote a detailed diary about the happenings in the palace. One day he proudly noted that his children were taking swimming lessons with the children of the pharaoh. What games do you suppose they played as they happily splashed in the beautiful Nile?

Some of the ancients swam in order to fight wars. Artists in Assyria drew pictures on stones showing their soldiers swimming away from an enemy who was pursuing them with a bow and arrow. The soldiers had made their own flotation devices out of animal skins filled with air. They supported themselves on these primitive air mattresses and paddled along, using their arms and legs in a way similar to our crawl stroke.

Of course, everyone knows that the Greeks and Romans were the first serious boosters of physical fitness. In fact, there were even laws requiring all the Spartan children to learn to swim. They evidently enjoyed it, for public baths were plentiful throughout Athens and Rome. Anyone could go for a swim for just a few pennies.

Caesar was so enthusiastic about the sport that he held swimming meets for his troops when they camped on river banks. Sometimes he led his men into battle across rivers and bays. They used an overhand stroke. (We know this from ancient coins showing the soldiers swimming into battle.)

And then there was Leander. Leander was a handsome young man of Greece. He was in love with a beautiful maiden, Hero. To be with her he had to swim across the Hellespont (a big bay). He did this frequently, but alas, he became careless and forgot to obey the safety rules. One stormy night he couldn't make it and drowned on the way to his beloved.

The missionaries who traveled into the South Seas couldn't believe their eyes when they saw the Polynesian babies swimming in blue waters of Polynesia, nor could they believe the amazing achievements of the pearl and sponge divers who swam to greet the ships as they arrived. They wrote home in wonder about the obvious enjoyment these people found in water activities.

My favorite historical story of swimming is about Benjamin Franklin. During the early days of our country, when he was in England representing us in court, most people thought that even bath water was bad for you and would make you sick. Hardly anyone actually swam. But Ben Franklin was different. He liked the water and on Sunday afternoons would go to the River Thames in London for a little dip. Sometimes he would put something like our modern scuba fins on his feet, paddles on his hands, and a kite on his back. What a strange sight he must have been! No wonder people gathered on the river banks to watch and begged him to teach them all to swim, too!

Question: Can big brothers and sisters be good instructors?
Answer: Yes, as long as they are happy, low-key people who are not inclined to be critical or to tease. Little kids love to do the same thing big kids do. As demonstrators, they are invaluable!

Question: My child doesn't seem to like swimming lessons. Should I let him quit?
Answer: Make sure your instructor is reliable, flexible, alert, and understanding. Then encourage your child and help in every way you can, including by making practice and play time available. Swimming is frequently the first difficult thing a child does, and for the sake of future confidence and habit I feel it is important to continue. Quitting when something is difficult can become a real cop-out. There was a student in one of my kindergarten classes who was determined to quit. She even figured out how to put her finger down her throat to make herself vomit as she waited her turn. It was hard to ignore her, but after a few days she gave up and learned to swim and have fun like her friends.

Question: What should I do about the water getting into my child's mouth when he swims?
Answer: Don't worry about it! It is fascinating that young babies love to feel the water in their mouths. Remind your child to hum and hold his breath, but even so he may keep water in his mouth. Some grownups do it, too. They close up the glottis and forget it.

Question: When is the best time to start my family in a swimming program?
Question: NOW! Be water-wise! You'll have fun—I'm positive!

Suggested Readings

Armbruster, David A., Robert H. Allen, and Robert S. Billingsley. *Swimming and Diving.* St. Louis, MO: C. V. Mosby Co., 1968.

Billingsley, Hobie. *Diving Illustrated.* New York: Ronald Press Co., 1965.

Bortstein, Larry, and Henry Berkowitz. *Scuba, Spear and Snorkel.* Chicago: Cowles Book Co., Inc., 1971.

Chapman, Charles F. *Piloting Seamanship and Small Boat Handling.* New York: Hearst Corp., 1975.

Cooper, Kenneth H., M.D.M.P.H. *The Aerobics Way.* Philadelphia: M. Evans and Co., 1977.

Council for National Cooperation in Aquatics. *Lifeguard Training, Principles and Administration.* New York: Association Press, 1968.

Council for National Cooperation in Aquatics. *Water Fun for Everyone.* New York: Association Press, 1965.

Counsilman, Dr. James E. *The Science of Swimming.* Englewood Cliffs, NJ: Prentice-Hall, 1968.

——. *The Complete Book of Swimming,* New York: Atheneum, 1977.

Foshee, John. *Alabama Canoe Rides and Float Trips.* Huntsville, AL: Strode Publishers, 1975.

Gabrielson, M. A., Spears, B., and Gabrielson, B. W. *Aquatics Handbook.* Englewood Cliffs, NJ: Prentice-Hall, 1960, 1968.

Kauffman, Carolyn. *How To Teach Children To Swim.* New York: G. P. Putnam's Sons, 1960.

Lanoue, Fred R. *Drownproofing: A New Technique for Water Safety.* Englewood Cliffs, NJ: Prentice-Hall, 1963.

Liebers, Arthur. *Encyclopedia of Pleasure Boating,* revised edition. Cranbury: NJ: A. S. Barnes and Co., 1968.

McCardle, Katch. *Nutrition, Weight Control and Exercise.* Boston: Houghton-Mifflin, 1977.

Miner, Maryalice. *Sing a Song of Swimming.* Privately published, 1975.

Morgan, Elaine. *Descent of Woman.* New York: Stein and Day, 1972.

Newman, Virginia Hunt. *Teaching an Infant to Swim.* New York: Harcourt, Brace and World, 1967.

Peppe, Mike. *Sports Illustrated Book of Diving.* Philadelphia: J. B. Lippincott, 1961.

Ryan, Jack. *Learning To Swim Is Fun.* New York: Ronald Press Co., 1960.

Spears, Betty. *Fundamentals of Synchronized Swimming.* Minneapolis, MN: Burgess Publishing Co., 1950.

Timmermans, Claire. *How To Teach Your Baby To Swim.* New York: Stein and Day, 1975.

Index